DANCING THE DREAM

DANCING THE DREAM

The First Nations and the Church in Partnership

Joyce Carlson, *Editor*

Illustrated by Teresa Altiman

ANGLICAN BOOK CENTRE
Toronto, Canada

DBN: 1328/75

1995
Anglican Book Centre
600 Jarvis Street
Toronto, Ontario
Canada M4Y 2J6

Illustrations: Teresa Altiman © 1995 the Council for Native Ministries
Book design, typesetting: Willem Hart Art & Design Inc.

All stories are used with the permission of the storytellers.

This book was commissioned by the Council for Native Ministries
of the Anglican Church of Canada in 1994.

Canadian Cataloguing in Publication Data

Main entry under title:

Dancing the dream : the First Nations and the church in partnership

ISBN 1-55126-105-7

1. Native peoples – Canada – Religion
I. Carlson, Joyce.

E78.C2D3 1995   306'.089'97071   C95-931709-0

For all children
who died while attending residential schools
and lie in unmarked graves
and for all who have experienced abuse
and who struggle to come to terms
with culture and identity

and to the memory of Dominic Eshkakagon

elder at the Dancing the Dream convocation
who had a special place in his heart for children
and whose wisdom played a significant role
in the evolution of that Anglican dream

Dominic passed away 9 October 1994

CONTENTS

FOREWORD

It was a moving experience for me to share in the Second National Native Convocation of our church, *Dancing the Dream.*

Reading these words brings back to me all the voices to which we listened during those important days.

It has been my privilege to share in both convocations. The first time I was the only non-Native partner; this time there were others. That is just one sign I see of increasing self-assurance in First Nation congregations and leaders, and I look forward to seeing even more such signs.

I am grateful to all who shared in planning and in carrying out the work of this event. It will long be remembered for its power and its beginnings of healing, and I especially will remember it in that way.

May God continue to heal, to strengthen, and to bless us in our task of serving the people and the world which God has made and redeemed in our Lord Jesus Christ.

Archbishop Michael G. Peers
Primate of the Anglican Church of Canada

PREFACE

In August 1993 I went to the second national convocation of Native and Inuit peoples from the Anglican Church of Canada at Minaki Lodge, Ontario. I was to write daily reports during the convocation and prepare a final report to serve as a permanent record. I was invited to be a participant-observer. In this role I attended all talks, worship services, and presentations. I participated in small groups and met with designated leaders.

I quickly learned that it was not possible to be a participant-observer. I participated fully. Like many others, I had an entirely sleepless night after the residential school sharing. At the end of the conference, my body ached. What set this apart from many other conferences I have attended in the past was that it struck very close to home in many ways.

I grew up in the area referred to as "Red River" by early missionaries. My own ancestors were among the mixed-race people who were married and had their children baptized by the first Anglican missionaries. I experienced Aboriginal values as positive although I did not really understand the culture out of which those values arose. They were little discussed, being undervalued by the local and the larger communities. At the convocation I was moved by symbols and imagery which gave insight into a spirituality deeply connected to the natural world—a relatedness to creation and Creator in ways I had not previously understood. I have had glimpses of this connectedness with creation in the past; but there I observed again and again the depth of the reverence for Creator, creation, and creatures revealed through actions and words of participants as they shared their hopes, dreams, and understandings of faith.

As a former child welfare worker and a parent, I felt a deep sadness at the loss in Aboriginal communities. The suicide rate among youth is six times the national average; many die violent deaths. I was greatly challenged by the cries of the youth. "Give us our voice," they said. And they meant it.

As a child I hated conflict. A part of my struggle was with the conflict between the values of the Aboriginal and the larger communities. Over the years I have come to understand that conflict is sometimes a necessary part of growth. One cannot suppress the pain to avoid the conflict. Confronting broken-ness may be uncomfortable, but it has the potential to bring wholeness. We have often heard *about* Aboriginal people from outsiders serving in their communities. Seldom have we heard the stories in the voices of Aboriginal people themselves. Their stories at the convocation brought a depth of pain; they also brought a beginning of healing. Amidst the tears were laughter and friendship.

Abuse is devastating. But there is a profound grace in experi-encing the love of God expressed through the community of faith. The church is the body of Christ; and when one part of the body hurts, we all hurt. We need each other if we are to come to wholeness, and we need to hear each other's stories if we are to heal.

The writing of the book began at the second convocation. In a larger sense, however, the book had its beginnings in the first contact of Native peoples with early church missionaries and in the differing cultural values and attitudes of European new-comers and First Nations peoples. And it is an ongoing story.

A few months after the second convocation, a group of Aboriginal Anglicans were invited to gather in April 1994 at a Partners in Mission consultation called to advise the church on priorities. Energized by the dream which had emerged at the convocation, these Native leaders agreed to work toward creation of "a new self-determining community within the Anglican church." This book is a response to the rapid changes that have taken place in a short time. It is an expansion of the original report: a record of the second convocation and a documentation of further steps taken to reach the historic decision ratified by the National Executive Council in May 1994.

The desire of Aboriginal peoples is for a new partnership. As Margaret Waterchief, a priest of the Siksika First Nation, has said, "We are all sisters and brothers in Christ, and we are called to be equal. We understand the problems of our own people, our own communities, in ways that many others don't because they haven't lived in our communities and don't understand our culture. We must take our place as equal partners in order to better serve our communities, to bring Christ's love to all."

Affirmation of the giftedness within Aboriginal cultures and communities serves to strengthen communities and bring Christ's love to all. My prayer is that this book will help us affirm and celebrate not only Aboriginal cultures but all the different expressions of culture within the Anglican communion. The celebration of cultural diversity has the potential to enrich our church. As we affirm the giftedness of all, we may all be made more whole, more complete. This is possible because our faith is in a loving God who calls us to fullness of life and unity.

Joyce Carlson

Editor's Note: The terminology in this book reflects the variety of terms used by First Nations people speaking of themselves. "Indigenous" is used universally to describe all First Nations peoples. Individuals may also describe themselves as "Aboriginal," "Native," and "Indian."

ACKNOWLEDGEMENTS

I am indebted to Laverne Jacobs, Lana Grawbarger, and James Isbister, who consulted on the formation of this book. Mervin Wolfleg, Donna Bomberry, and Vi Smith assisted with corrections. Special thanks go to Vi Samaha and Elders of her home community for assistance in the final reading. Doug Tindal offered recommendations about design and read first and second drafts. John Bird and Murray Still assisted with reporting at the convocation, and John offered comments. Teresa Mandricks provided administrative assistance. Special thanks are also due Robert Maclennan, of the Anglican Book Centre, for encouragement and Ginny Arthur for careful editing.

All participants courageously shared their stories at the convocation. Their stories are used here with permission. Dale Ahenakew, a young man who led my small group, showed great compassion. In traditional cultures "Keepers of the Memory" had a role of "remembering"—of bringing teachings of the past into the present and holding them for the future. Daily the leaders provided reflections long into the evenings. I appreciated all Elders. Their reflections modeled true Eldership rooted in a long tradition of respecting all.

I was delighted when the Council for Native Ministries invited Teresa Altiman of Walpole Island First Nation to prepare art. Teresa was particularly touched by the story of a young girl whose hair was cut off upon entering residential school. Aware that cutting of hair is associated with death and mourning in Aboriginal communities, Teresa felt the story expressed poignantly the inner death and mourning that many have felt in being separated from families and communities. Each illustration is a sensitive reflection of her own soul searching and desire to participate in the healing process, not only for those directly affected by the residential school experience but also for the next generations whose lives may continue to be affected. Her offering of her time and creative energy in preparation of the art is a gift.

Much grief was expressed at the convocation; and in writing

this book, I felt particularly close to three children whose lives have touched mine deeply. The first is my childhood playmate and sister whose illness and institutionalization at the age of ten brought an awareness of the anguish of separation. The second is my brother who died tragically at the age of twelve. The third is our first child, whose suffering and death ultimately brought me closer to a loving God.

Within my diocesan community I am indebted to Ralph Baxter, a friend and an encouragement in writing, and to Leyah McFadyen, a companion on my journey. My lively junior high Sunday school class at St. Margaret's parish constantly challenge my perception of church. I appreciate the insights of Gladys Cook, Phyllis Keeper, and Mina Stevenson, who participated in a small group in our diocese. I am grateful to Bishop Pat Lee, Carol Throp, and Judy Bjerring for encouragement.

Stan McKay and Alf Dumont of the Liturgical Resources Project affirmed the importance of the work. Brian Bjerring, Anne Davidson, Kathleen Schmidt, and Sue Moxley offered insight and suggestions.

I have a great respect for Michael Peers, for his vision of unity and gentle spirit.

My husband Len and my children Karen, Andrea, and Ian have taught me much about living with kindness and celebrating the power of love in the world.

Joyce Carlson

1 / A VISION OF PARTNERSHIP

The histories of the Indigenous peoples and of the Anglican Church of Canada have been interwoven since their first contact, and each has had a profound impact upon the other. Many people are aware of this historic connection. Less clear may be the variety of cultural expressions within Indigenous communities across Canada, the Territories, and the Arctic and the profoundly negative impact of undervaluing those cultures in the larger society as well as in the churches. There are at least eleven major cultural groups and up to fifty-three different languages. While there are differences among Indigenous peoples, there are many similarities: in world view, in relationships within families, and in understandings of community and of relatedness to creation. It is important to understand that the cultures of all Native and Inuit peoples are very different from European-based cultures.

The confrontation between European and Indigenous cultures is particularly evident in painful experiences described by those who were sent as children to church-run residential schools. The residential school system was set up as a part of the policy of the Canadian government to assimilate First Nations peoples into a society based on European values. The view that it was desirable to change Indigenous cultures often existed alongside the desire to spread the gospel of Christ, and residential schools seemed to be a means of addressing both objectives. The result has been untold pain and grief for those who experienced the implementation of this policy and who continue to live with the aftermath.

This book documents a journey toward the healing of this pain and grief and the resulting changed relationship of Indigenous peoples with the Anglican Church of Canada. This new relationship is expressed in a covenant signed by twenty leaders at a gathering of Native Anglicans at a special Partners in Mission consultation held in April 1994. These leaders called for the creation of a truly Indigenous Anglican church in Canada to function in partnership with the present Anglican Church.

THE COVENANT

We representatives of Indigenous people of the Anglican Church of Canada, meeting in Winnipeg from the 23 to 26 of April, 1994, pledge ourselves to this covenant for the sake of our people and in trust of our Lord and saviour, Jesus Christ:

Under the guidance of God's spirit we agree to do all we can do to call our people into unity in a new, self-determining community within the Anglican Church of Canada.

To this end, we extend the hand of partnership to all those who will help us build a truly Anglican Indigenous Church in Canada.

May God bless this new vision and give us grace to accomplish it.

Amen

This invitation to partnership was affirmed by the National Executive Council of the Anglican Church of Canada on May 5, 1994, in Winnipeg.

Moved by: Caleb Lawrence
Seconded by: Vi Samaha

That this National Executive Council acknowledges and welcomes the invitation of representatives of the indigenous people of the Anglican Church of Canada, meeting in Winnipeg from the 23rd to 26th of April 1994, to call the indigenous people into unity in a new, self-determining community within the Anglican Church of Canada, refers the invitation to the Council for Native Ministries, and pledges its prayerful support and dialogue throughout this process of developing that relationship.

This changed relationship has been brought about by the ongoing work in the last twenty-five years of many people within the Aboriginal community and with the support and encouragement of the whole Anglican Church of Canada. Aboriginal leaders have met at two major convocations, *Sharing the Dream* in 1988 and *Dancing the Dream* in 1993. Events of these two convocations increased the confidence and voice of Aboriginal peoples.

At the second convocation in August 1993, the primate of the Anglican Church of Canada offered an apology to the Native peoples for the church's role in the abuses of the residential schools. Donna Bomberry, from the Cayuga Nation (Iroquois Confederacy), chairperson of the Council for Native Ministries, described the apology as an especially enabling moment. A great deal of pain had emerged as delegates shared what the experience of residential schools had meant in their lives. Many people felt relief when the church, through the primate's apology, acknowledged its own role in this pain. Following the convocation, much reflection and soul searching led nine months later, at the consultation in Winnipeg, to a real clarity around the need for self-determination. The covenant and invitation to partnership reflected a changed relationship with the Anglican Church.

Donna reflects on the development of this new relationship as follows:

A NEW RELATIONSHIP
by Donna Bomberry

When I heard the primate say the words, "I am sorry . . . that we tried to re-make you in our image. . . ," the words rang very clear and true.

This acknowledgment by the church helped me to set my mind to the future. I wondered, "How do I receive this? What is the next step?"

As I considered his words, I found that he helped to encapsulate so many of the struggles we've had. Within the Aboriginal community we've always acknowledged that we do things differently, that we see things differently. We have always tried to fit into a hierarchy and a structure which is foreign to us (it has never really been suited to us culturally), and we have failed. We have tried to fit in and we have failed.

When I reflected on the apology, I felt deeply: Yes, that is what has happened. Yes, we agree on this, and a part of our work as members of the Anglican church is to be self-determining people. We need to identify the way we work and the way we see things differently.

The apology was an enormously freeing moment which released us from that image of being boxed into and failing at trying to live up to something that was wrong for us. The image simply did not fit for us. It wasn't us. It wasn't based on our experience. In the months following the convocation, I reflected on the primate's statement, "I am sorry that we tried to remake you in our image," and continued to "feel with" what that meant in our lives spiritually. I knew that this was our struggle: the image of what it is to be Christian and Aboriginal is different from what was presented to us and what we had tried unsuccessfully to live.

We are a praying people. We always use Traditional and Christian teachings to guide our prayer and reflections; so we used biblical understanding of scriptures as well as our Aboriginal teachings to try to discern how we could assist the structure in visioning the church into the next century.

It became clear to us that we have different issues. We have different ways of being church. At our consultation when we were asked to help the church determine what it could look like in the next century, we reflected on the last century. Clearly the structure and the image of church which we had tried to live within did not fit. We all knew that immediately, and we dared to vision.

Our vision is a vision of who we are as God's people. It is not concrete, but it is our claiming our place as equal partners in the church. As this vision grows and develops, we become more confident as Christian people. We have much to offer our own people if given the opportunity. We have much to offer the rest of the church as well. Our decision to be self-determining was so unanimous, so incredible! It was a mutual, natural next step after the apology. We simply declared it.

From now on, when we look at where we fit in the structure, we see ourselves as a partner in this church and as a self-determining body. We now need to use our own spirituality to describe our faith in our own way. All things have to be developed, stated, and understood so that we feel we are truly part of the church. . . . We are not on the outside any more.

This book documents the steps which resulted in the radical reconception by Aboriginal peoples of themselves, and the resulting changed relationship of Indigenous peoples to the national Anglican Church. It documents the thoughtful approach to the first convocation, which Native people planned themselves. Their careful steps to affirming their own cultural tradition reflect the depth of a spirituality they began to recover and explore. While some parts of their Traditional spirituality have been retained in more remote communities, many Aboriginal spiritual ceremonies have been discouraged for generations. Not until the fifties and sixties did Aboriginal spiritual ceremonies begin to be practiced more openly.

Many First Nations peoples embraced the gospel and took it to their hearts. Some left Traditional ways and culture. Others attempted to integrate their own understandings with the Christian. Many have struggled over generations with what it has meant to be Christian and Aboriginal. The recovery and exploration of Aboriginal culture and spiritual traditions has led to a confrontation with some of the oppression experienced by Aboriginal peoples. For many, the experience of attending church-run residential schools produced a traumatic loss of language and culture. Far from their families, many experienced physical, sexual, emotional, and spiritual abuses. The impact of these church-run residential school experiences will be felt by First Nations communities for generations.

The greater part of this book is dedicated to events of the second convocation, *Dancing the Dream*, which built upon the learnings of the first. The event was both a celebration and a challenge: it was a celebration of the spirituality of a people as they began to embrace it; it was a challenge to others to understand, honour, and affirm that spirituality. It is a spirituality little known in the larger church. The speakers and sharing at *Dancing the Dream* assisted us in understanding why so little was known or understood about First Nations people and pointed us in a direction more inclusive of First Nations people. Perhaps this account will help us also to listen to the voices of many others who have often not been heard in the Anglican communion.

First Nations Anglicans desire to share their faith experiences with the larger church. We hope they will point to new ways of being the church together. In the following pages you will learn the history which led to the convocations. Talks by leaders at the event and reflections of First Nations participants, as well as of non-Native participants and of international partners, helped us understand the dialogue already taking place. The presence of international partners was significant at the *Dancing the Dream* convocation and at the later consultation which resulted in the covenant and decision to form a new partnership. International partners affirmed that the movement of Indigenous peoples to autonomy and self-determination is worldwide. The appendix of this book contains a collection of prayers and an exercise based on a ceremony from the 1992 Anglican Encounter in Brazil; these may be used by persons wishing to begin healing groups within their communities or by parishes wishing to understand more about First Nations members in our communion.

There has been enormous growth among First Nations leaders and community members. First Nations people are at different places in their own growth, but there is a real affirmation of the need for dialogue and exploration of differing understandings. The book draws us into the First Nations' vision of the future and assists us in understanding their past. The stories shared, the history of the relationships, the reflections—all these may assist us in moving through the painful moments of sharing the depth of the hurt to the celebration of the giftedness of First Nations peoples across Canada, who form an important and distinct part of our communion. Their gifts, freely shared, enrich all members of the Anglican Church of Canada.

2 / SHARING THE DREAM

Within First Nations communities dreams are connected to, and a reflection of, a deep spirituality. Planners of the first national Native convocation held in Fort Qu'Appelle, Saskatchewan, in 1988, chose the theme *Sharing the Dream* to affirm their spirituality and to symbolize their desire to share it with the larger church.

Lana Grawbarger from Garden River First Nation (Ojibwe), a member of the Council for Native Ministries and great granddaughter of Chief Shinwaulk, a widely respected Ojibwe Christian leader, described the dream of First Nations people in this way: "We want to be accepted fully as we are, not as someone would want us to be. We have gifts. We want to celebrate those gifts and offer them."

With the exception of the primate, that first gathering was restricted to Native participants. They felt it was important to draw together to consider their own identity without intrusion. They wanted to be able to say, "This is our voice. This is the way we vision the work of the Holy Spirit, the Christian Church within our communities." The question they were asking was: *What may we offer the Anglican Church of Canada?*

They structured that gathering around their dream of being recognized for their own unique giftedness. Respect for others and an honouring of all creation are consistent values within the community. Through their Christian experience these First Nations people had a sense of being a part of one body, the body of the larger church. In their own tradition they believed it was important to pay respect to and acknowledge First Nations people in the area in which they were meeting, the Qu'Appelle valley.

The Qu'Appelle valley was formed as the last glaciers receded

Who is Calling

from the plains thousands of years ago. When they melted, the mighty glaciers carved a deep valley. As one drives across the plains of Saskatchewan, the valley suddenly opens ahead. In late summer, the surrounding fields are often brown and gold, approaching harvest; but the valley is green. In First Nations tradition green is the colour of kindness; like grass, no matter how many times you cut it, it keeps coming back.

Gently sloping hills reach up from the sides of the valley. Berry bushes and shrubbery grow in the gulleys. At the centre of the valley are the "Spirit Lakes." The word *Qu'Appelle* is a direct French translation of the Cree word *Pawkwa* meaning "Who is calling?" The Qu'Appelle has always been a sacred place among Plains people. A legend describes the origin of the name.

Many years ago a young woman and her three children were crossing the lake when the ice was not yet firm. They fell through and were lost. Over the years as people camped in the area, they believed they sometimes heard voices crying. They whispered to each other, "Who is calling? Who is calling?"

Legends and symbols reveal a deep sense of connectedness to creation and the Creator. This connectedness leads to a corresponding care for creation which is critically needed in our world. Such understandings of First Nations peoples are quietly held and form a unique world view. It is a gift, a part of the offering of Aboriginal peoples. The symbols, deep spirituality, and profound connectedness to creation were evident from the beginning in the planning of the Qu'Appelle event.

Elders from the First Nations community of Standing Buffalo, near the Qu'Appelle Valley, were invited to open the gathering. The symbol they used was the sacred pipe, a symbol of completeness. The elements forming the pipe are wood and stone, representing masculine and feminine aspects of our being. There is a oneness in the symbols of tree and rock. The union of the symbols as they come together in the formation of the pipe represents life itself.

The Elders shared the pipe in a circle, a symbol of wholeness. They offered thanks for their families and for their communities and offered a blessing and prayer of support for the convocation. The pipe within First Nations tradition has also been symbolic of a solemn promise or agreement. Eva Solomon, an Ojibwe (Roman Catholic) nun, describes the impor-

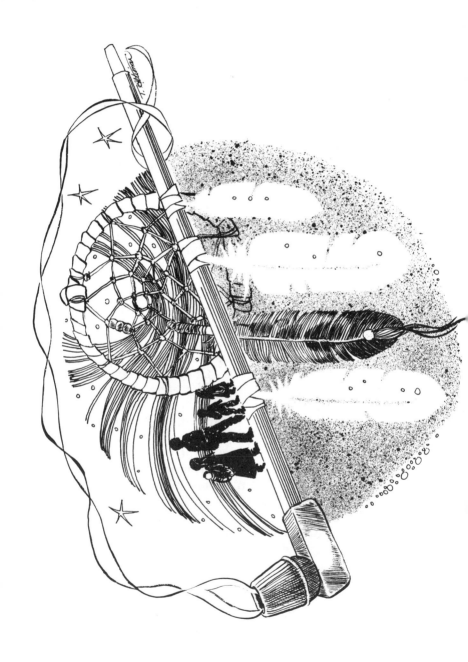

tance of the sacred pipe at that first Convocation.

THE SACRED PIPE
by Eva Solomon

If we search with good faith, with integrity, God will be with us. God will be with us in whatever way that will be. God promises, "If you seek me with all your heart, I will let you find me."

That is God's promise to us. If we seek God with integrity and love, we do not have to fear because God's power is with us. *spirit (church)*

God gave all people ways to come to know God. God's son was given for the whole world. God could have chosen the Aboriginal peoples of North America, but God chose the Hebrew people of Judea. *because they were blind.*

All are part of the same whole. We all come from one God. We choose the good parts of the spirituality of our ancestors who had their own ways of coming to God.

The pipe brings together all of us—and all the elements of the earth. The bowl of the pipe is made of our mother earth, stone; the stem is made of wood and is decorated with different things; in some areas it is covered with sage. The bowl represents truth. The stem represents honesty, the straight road the Creator has called us to walk.

In sharing the pipe we sometimes place it on our heads or on our hearts. In doing so we are making a covenant with each other. We are saying that we will be one with each other.

Closeness to creation and sensitivity to surroundings led to painful moments at the gathering. In addition to being a place of sacredness to Plains peoples, the Qu'Appelle Valley is home to a sanatorium in which many First Nations peoples died of tuberculosis. Made obsolete by new treatments for the disease, the old sanatorium has been converted into a conference centre. The convocation met in this very centre. It was chosen because it could accommodate a large number of people, but the memories for many were painful.

Tuberculosis epidemics of past generations took a particularily high toll on First Nations peoples. Although they had medicines for many diseases, they had no previous experience of tuberculosis. Their own medicines did not help them; there was no known cure. Many people were sent to the sanatorium with the

Sharing the Dream

hope of a recovery; but also, because tuberculosis was a highly communicable disease, isolation was recommended for the sake of the rest of the community. Lodging the convocation in this place, where a disproportionately high number of First Nations people had died away from homes and families, brought an acute awareness of loss.

This loss, according to James Isbister, past chairperson of the Council for Native Ministries, was symbolic of the enormous losses people had suffered over the years in their own spirituality and tradition. That the reclaiming and recovery of their dream should take place in a centre so symbolic of pain and loss speaks of the strength of their spirits.

At that first convocation the emphasis on *dream* was empowering. One day Rose Evans of Norway House shared a dream she had the previous night:

I saw a beautiful feather coming out of the sky . . . and I didn't want it to touch the ground. I was going to catch it. . . . And all of a sudden it was pulled up. My people were trying to get the feather and they were trying to reach the feather, but others were controlling it. The people wanted the feather so much because it meant so much to them. Everything is sacred to them. The feather was symbolic of the dream of my people to stand together, to help each other, to pray for each other and to have strength. . . .

Sharing the Dream, a pentecostal experience for First Nations people, brought a vibrant renewal, a reclaiming of spirituality and connectedness to Traditional understandings. This renewal has drawn many more First Nations people into the church and has given renewed hope to those already there. It has also been a source of increasing stress within the community as some people reclaimed their heritage and faced some of the painful experiences which had caused them to deny it.

Others viewed this attempt to recover heritage and culture with fear and suspicion because they have favoured the more traditional Christianity brought by missionaries. There has been a rift about spirituality at a time when the communities have been in crisis, attempting to deal with disproportionately high rates of unemployment and death due to suicide and violence. The rate of unemployment stands at between 70 percent and 80 percent for most communities. The suicide rate among youth ages sixteen to twenty-four is six times the national average.

While there was considerable pain within the Aboriginal community about reclaiming and affirming past spiritual understandings and practices, the approach of the larger church was "to listen." The primate, Michael Peers, was the only non-Native among the 180 people at the first convocation. He emphasized the importance of listening to the experience of First Nations people. His attitude of listening pointed to the new relationship between the church and First Nations people, a relationship which had been altered dramatically since the political changes of the sixties and the Hendry Report, which was commissioned by General Synod and presented in 1969.

3 / NATIVE PEOPLES AND SOVEREIGNTY
   WITHIN THE CHURCH

Laverne Jacobs, Coordinator of Native Ministries, is a member of Walpole Island First Nation. He cherishes the memory of a strong relationship with his grandmother, an enormously spiritual woman who was cared for by his parents. Confined to her bed in her final years, she had a profound impact on Laverne's spiritual formation. Many Aboriginal youth have had similar experiences.

His community of Walpole Island in the St. Clair River had remained separate and autonomous until Laverne's generation. Native peoples received the right to vote in 1960. The sixties brought many cultural and political changes for Native people. Laverne's family was politically very involved during those turbulent times of change. In 1967 his father, Burton Jacobs, made Walpole Island the first self-governing Native community in Canada. Now an Elder, Burton served as Chief of Walpole Island Reserve for five consecutive terms and as a councillor for over forty years.

Laverne, one of five siblings, suffered recurring illness as a child. He was strengthened and upheld through this adversity by the faith of his family. His mother, a graduate of teacher's college, encouraged him to continue his education. She sacrificed a great deal to ensure continuing opportunities for her children.

Immediately after high school, Laverne worked in a bank for a number of years before following his call into the ministry. Laverne enjoyed writing and communicating, excelling in English and literature in university. He was ordained in 1975 and served in parishes at Walpole Island, Forest, and Kettle Point for thirteen years before joining the national staff of the Anglican Church in 1987.

Since joining national staff, Laverne's emphasis has been to affirm the rich spiritual traditions of First Nations members of the Anglican Church of Canada. He provided this chapter which is based on a report to the Royal Commission on Aboriginal Peoples in November 1993.

At General Synod of 1965 the Anglican Church of Canada began to look at its relationship with Native peoples. In 1967 at General Synod, the Anglican Church went on record in support of Native self-determination and commissioned a study of the church's relationship with Native peoples. This study was undertaken by Dr. Charles Hendry and was presented to General Synod in 1969.

In his report *Beyond Traplines*, Hendry challenged the church to respond to the following recommendations:

1. The church must listen to the Native peoples.
2. The church must clarify its basic intentions.
3. The role of the church must be redefined.
4. The church must redeploy its resources.
5. The church must vitalize its education for ministry.
6. The church must develop strategies looking toward basic innovation.

General Synod gave approval to the recommendations of the Hendry Report and encouraged its implementation at various levels within the church. This was a pivotal moment in the church's relationship with Native peoples; it marked the beginning of a move away from colonialism and paternalism toward a more equal partnership.

Some concrete signs of the church's intentions were the employment of a full-time national staff person in 1969 as Consultant on Native Affairs and the establishment of the Subcommittee on Native Affairs in 1973. Together, the staff person and subcommittee played an intermediary role relaying Native issues to the church.

During this period in the seventies, Native people within the church were wrestling with identity and developing a sense of community among themselves. Progress was not entirely satisfactory. The Subcommittee on Native Affairs had little power; it was a sub-committee of the Program Committee without direct access to the National Executive Council.

In 1980 the Subcommittee on Native Affairs was reconstituted as the Council on Native Affairs (CNA) and became a standing committee of General Synod reporting directly to the National Executive Council. Native peoples now had a much stronger voice within the decision-making structure of the church.

This new council began to work toward increased involvement in the life and structures of the church. The council began to push for Native representation on various committees. In 1983 two members of Council on Native Affairs were appointed to the Primate's World Relief and Development Fund. In 1985 one Council on Native Affairs member was appointed to the board of the Canadian Council of Churches. In 1985 eight young Native people were delegates to the Anglican Church's National Youth Conference, which led to the appointment of one Native youth to the Youth Unit of the Anglican Church of Canada. In 1986 two Native people were elected to the National Executive Council, the Anglican Church's highest legislative body between sessions of General Synod. One member of Council on Native Affairs was elected to the Program Committee.

The Council on Native Affairs and Native members of committees of the church focused much of their energy on enlisting the support of the church in advocacy for Native issues, particularly land claims and recognition of Native sovereignty by the various levels of government in Canada. This work addressed social justice issues in Canadian society and occurred largely outside the church. The task of enlisting support and educating the church constituency was a difficult and lonely responsibility.

During the latter half of the eighties, the council began to take a close look at itself and at Native political organizations. Native organizations, including the council, were becoming more Westernized, adopting the philosophy, ways, and values of Euro-Canadian society. Many Native political leaders were making politics their goal and losing touch with their own communities. This development was disturbing; even more disturbing was the realization that these leaders appeared to be neglecting their own rich spiritual heritage.

The council had been cautioned by Elders, their spiritual leaders, not to lose their spiritual roots and heritage. Council members understood the wisdom of this advice and began a process of recovery of spirituality. This has become the work of the nineties.

A shift in focus occurred. Aware that any process of recovery must begin with self and must focus on social justice issues within the church, the council moved to work within the church itself—rather than addressing concerns to government and Canadian society. This shift in focus was marked by a change in name from *Council on Native Affairs* to *Council for Native Ministries* (CNM) and the staff position changed from *Consultant on Native Affairs* to *Coordinator of Native Ministries.*

During this period of introspection in the late eighties, an historic and pentecostal event took place for Native peoples. A convocation was held in Fort Qu'Appelle, Saskatchewan, from September 28 to October 8, 1988. It was a time of affirmation and empowerment. The convocation brought together 180 Native Canadian Anglicans to share their experiences and dreams as Native peoples and as members of the Anglican Church of Canada.

This gathering recommended that the General Synod and the National Executive Council authorize a second convocation and enable participation of Native peoples in all aspects of the church. Further, the gathering initiated a process of rediscovery and affirmation of Native heritage; there began an exploration of identities of First Nations peoples, who began to discern the confusion of internalized misconceptions imposed by the dominant society.

The Council for Native Ministries commenced implementation of the resolution to General Synod regarding Native self-expression in the Church:

That this General Synod . . . is resolved to respond to "the desire on the part of Christians of the Native Peoples of the Anglican Church of Canada for a greater degree of self-expression both in the services of the Church, and control and government of the work of the church among the Native Peoples of Canada, and more particularly, how to incorporate into the work of the church the ideals, hopes and aspirations of the Native Peoples of Canada for their future."

That accordingly, this General Synod calls on all dioceses and parishes to review the forms of participation of the Indian Peoples of their diocese with a view to improving their participation. (1989)

The mandates arising from the convocation resulted in even more self-examination. The council found itself embroiled in difficult discussions around process and style of meeting. Members questioned whether to continue to use parliamentary procedure or to move to consensus decision making. One young man made a passionate plea:

I think that it should be out of respect that I stand. I had a hard time yesterday. I felt I was carrying a big load. My chest was heavy; and my mind. I didn't want to interfere with anybody. I was feeling that I had to be somebody that I didn't want to be. I respect the consensus decision-making process in the circle which is sacred. . . . I am open to the consensus model and to the sacred aspect of decision-making of the circle. I join you here as a representative of Living Waters and as a young person of Keewatin. It gives me the opportunity to participate as the person I am and not the person I'm expected to be. I respect myself as a Native person —how I think and make decisions as a Native person.

. . . We are very important leaders to our people. We should be example of *being Native people*; we should be the first to stand up to the structure [and say] that this is how we want to make decisions. Why did God make things in a circle? Native people who are close to nature and close to their Creator—we do things in a circle. I was uncomfortable with the way things are set up here. You have to look sideways to see who is talking. What I see here is, I think we should try and communicate to the system how we want and like to make decisions. I support the model suggested. I think we should not depend on numbers for quorum but that those here will make the decision. When we come to the celebration I want us to celebrate in the Native way. The system should start to change; let it start with us.

In May 1990 the Council for Native Ministries decided to abandon parliamentary procedure and return to the decision-making model of their ancestors—consensus—and to inform the National Executive Council of this decision.

The struggle around identity was focused in discussions of inculturation and integration of Native spirituality and Christianity. Council for Native Ministries members agonized over: *What does it mean to be Native and Christian? Can Native people embrace both traditions? Is Native spirituality compatible with Christianity?* Our Elders in the past told us that they put these pagan traditions aside and that it is wrong to take them up again. Having re-established the circle as an important cultural tradition, the question then became: *Is there room in the Circle for Traditional people and Christian people?*

The council asked the National Executive Council for a statement on Native spirituality and sponsored an ecumenical gathering of Native people from various communities. Participants included Traditional Elders, and Anglican, Roman Catholic, and United Church members. Together they shared their faith journeys and addressed the questions: *What does it mean to be Native and Christian? What is Native spirituality?* Insights from this dialogue were taken to National Executive Council. In spring 1992 the National Executive Council passed a resolution affirming the value of Native spirituality and encouraging Native members of the church to continue the dialogue on Native spirituality.

At that gathering of Native people discussing Native spirituality, it became abundantly clear that the root of much confusion and struggle with identity and Native spirituality could be attributed to the residential school system. Many mourned the loss of their languages and described severe punishments for speaking their languages. Others spoke about religious confusion.

The suffering of many in church-run residential schools came to public attention in 1990 when the Grand Chief of the Assembly of Manitoba Chiefs disclosed his personal abuse in a residential school. The primate of the Anglican Church of Canada received a request from a tribal council in Manitoba asking for redress and support from the church in dealing with the abuses which occurred through the residential school system.

The Council for Native Ministries worked closely with a task group to try to respond to this request. The council firmly believed that responsibility for addressing residential school abuses was the work of the whole church and resisted pressure to assume responsibility for this task. Council members maintained that to take responsibility themselves was like asking victims to be responsible for their own abuse.

The Council for Native Ministries worked very closely with the Residential School Task Force to facilitate a presentation on residential schools to the National Executive Council in May 1991. Council for Native Ministries arranged for two survivors of the residential schools to share their residential school experience with National Executive Council. Care was taken to provide appropriate orientation and introduction to the issue so that National Executive Council members would understand the need to respect the storytellers. The moving presentation resulted in the establishment of the Residential Schools Working Group, the hiring of staff, and the provision of sufficient funding to enable the church to respond to the cry for healing and redress.

During this process the Council for Native Ministries was growing in confidence, experiencing a real sense of identity and affirmation as First Nations peoples. This new confidence and growth exhibited itself in a number of ways. On one occasion, the council felt that plans for an event focusing on issues in First Nations communities were being made without consultation or involvement of Native people. When Council for Native Ministries took exception to this process and communicated its concern strongly, the original planning team was replaced with Native people named by the Council for Native Ministries.

This was a painful but necessary step in breaking down old patterns of paternalism and colonialism. To prevent this situation from being repeated the council presented and succeeded in having a resolution passed at the National Executive Council meeting:

That this NEC of the Anglican Church of Canada ensures that before any action is taken or policy adopted by the General Synod of the Anglican Church of Canada on any issue affecting Native Peoples, there will be consultation with the Council For Native Ministries and, where possible, Native persons will be included in the implementation of any such action or development of any such policy.

Shortly after this directive was passed, a Native appointment was made to the "Beginner's Group" as part of the General Synod strategic planning process. The appointment was made without consultation with the Council for Native Ministries, but the council later persuaded National Executive Council to ask Council for Native Ministries to name an additional Native person to the "Beginner's Group."

When funding was required for Living Waters, a Native branch of the Youth Unit, a request for allocation of funds to enable this group to meet was presented to the National Executive Council. The National Executive Council responded by directing a portion of the Council for Native Ministries budget to Living Waters. The Council for Native Ministries immediately introduced a resolution, ultimately successful, directing National Executive Council to rescind the motion and allocate new monies to meet the request from Living Waters.

The growing confidence of the Council for Native Ministries was dramatically visible at the 1992 General Synod of the Anglican Church of Canada. Through the efforts of the Council for Native Ministries, drums and Native elements and rituals were used in worship and presentations at General Synod. For the first time in the history of the Anglican Church, General Synod resolutions were presented in Native languages. A powerful educational event employing story, song, choreography, and a gift-giving moved people to tears. Resolutions were introduced calling for recognition and use of different ways of meeting, (i.e. consensus and the Circle); evaluation and accountability of all resolutions pertaining to Native peoples since the Hendry Report; and ongoing dialogue regarding Native spirituality. This was a synod which will be remembered for the powerful presence and impact of First Nations people. A foundation had been laid on which to build a new relationship.

4 / DANCING THE DREAM

Look to your people.
Look more closely at the gifts of your people;
they are beautiful.

Bert McKay
(Nisga'a First Nation)

As I hear many stories of my people I think of a symphony:
the violin cannot be an oboe; the oboe cannot be a clarinet—they are
not meant to be.

So it is with us:
each of us praise God in our own individual way—and there is
beauty to that.
There are many different voices,
there are many different melodies,
and they fit together and blend in beautiful ways.

This is the gift that we have been given,
and we are to respect the sound of the song
and the voices of the other players.

What we are doing now is learning how to play together;
We are learning to make a beautiful sound unto God.

Laverne Jacobs
(Walpole Island First Nation)

A t *Dancing the Dream*, the second convocation of Aboriginal peoples from across the Anglican Church of Canada at Minaki Lodge, Ontario, in 1993, another major step was made in developing a new relationship. At this event the 147 participants included ten non-Native members appointed by the church's National Executive Council. Their role was to listen and to find ways to convey their experience to the larger church.

Within Aboriginal tradition dance has always been linked to healing. *Dancing the Dream* was chosen as the title of the second convocation because of awareness in the community of the need to move in the direction of healing. Having been encouraged to affirm their own giftedness and spiritual roots, the people wished to share these gifts more widely in the Anglican Church of Canada and to celebrate them.

Planning for the second convocation began early in 1990, about the same time that the church began to deal with the impact that the residential schools had had on the lives of several generations of First Nations people. It was clear from the start that the misunderstandings between Aboriginal culture and the wider church would be most clearly visible in the confrontation of cultures which occurred for many children taken from their own homes and placed in church-run residential schools. Aware that the residential schools issue would be a painful topic, especially for any participants who had not previously had an opportunity to deal with their experiences, convocation planners considered with great care how to encourage sharing and begin healing.

Stan McKay, moderator of the United Church of Canada from 1992 to 1994 and originally from Fisher River First Nation in Manitoba, was present at some of the early planning to deal with abuses within the residential school system in the Anglican Church. Stan, then occupying his church's highest elected position, was later to disclose his own abuse at a church-run school. He stated, "From the very start of the planning, it was clear that healing was to involve everyone. The church is a community; and if one suffers, everyone suffers. The gospel is about wholeness of the people of God; healing is for everyone."

At the invitation of the Diocese of Keewatin, the second convocation took place at Minaki Lodge, the only conference site in Keewatin large enough to accommodate the high numbers expected to attend. The word *minaki* means "beautiful place" in the

Ojibwe language. Situated in the Lake of the Woods area in north-western Ontario, the lodge has been a well-known recreation area for many years; but few people within the Native community had been guests.

James Isbister, past chairperson of the Council for Native Ministries, had a profound awareness of the difficulty of meeting in this place.

All around us were the stuffed bodies of animals. These animals have been our livelihood, and we were taught always to treat them with respect. Here, they were mounted as trophies, lining the walls and standing in the lounges and hallways. Stuffed, they are empty. They are without life. What is there when there is no life? There is no spirit. To me, those stuffed trophies all around us were symbols of the loss of spirit within our communities—and thus were directly connected to the residential school issues.

It is important to have education; it was important for our people to have education. If they had had the education offered within their own communities where they could sift it and use their own wisdom to find what was helpful, we might have been able to really benefit; but to force children to be taken away and placed in institutions and to take away their language and culture was to take away their spirits. When you take away the spirit, you are left with broken spirits, broken people. That is the problem in our communities today. There are many broken spirits.

The first convocation had begun with a pipe ceremony, a symbol of the need to share. The convocation task force believed it was important to open the second convocation with an honour song, a traditional song that used a drum. James Isbister explains, "The drum is the heartbeat of Mother Earth. In order to dance, to celebrate our spirituality, we had to have a drum."

Convocation planners invited local Elder Roy McDonald of White Dog Reserve near Minaki to offer prayers in traditional Aboriginal style using a drum. He shared that in his own life he had had many disappointments, many hurts. Rejected by his parents, he was raised by grandparents. A return to his Traditional roots brought balance and hope in his life. He prayed that at the convocation the children of the future would be helped. His prayer closed with these words:

I am searching for my life. We must remember that in our times of struggle, we are making a path for our children.

There is a teaching of seven stars in our tradition. Three stars in a row represent the past; a middle one represents the present; three stars in a row represent the future.

The path we are trying to find now is a road for our youngsters.
As we find the path upon which to walk, we will be able to look back and know where we have come from.

Then, our children can also look back to know where they are from. When they know where they are from, they can look forward and see where they are going.

I give thanks for the opportunity to share, to speak about the purpose in everything. I sing a song of vision, a dream about my search for life.

Throughout the convocation, a Roman Catholic deacon and Elder, Dominic Eshkakagon, was present as Elder. With his experience in the Roman Catholic Church, he upheld Christian teachings. With his understanding of Traditional ways, he offered those traditions where they were helpful. He led gently and with a deep awareness of moments to enable others to speak, moments to draw the youth together, and moments of profound sharing.

The convocation task force wished to use colour and visual images to celebrate the spirituality and giftedness of all First Nations peoples. The main meeting room was filled with symbols of Christian and Aboriginal Tradition: some separate, some integrated in beautifully beaded patterns. Brightly coloured cloths symbolising the Four Directions, a teaching of First Nations people, were draped behind the altar.

A central question was: *How does one honour both the unique spiritual path of the people and the Christian faith?* This issue had been a source of pain and stress within the community. Many people now find they are upheld by understandings of the Christian faith; others, of the Tradition. Some are now integrating the two. At the convocation each day began and ended with worship led by First Nations peoples from many parts of the country and of differing cultural traditions.

First Nations cultures have historically been carried in an oral tradition. Teachings were passed by word of mouth in the circle. The planners wished to honour that tradition as well as to provide a record of daily events for participants to share with their home communities. Events of the day were discussed with reflective people called Keepers of the Memory, whose thoughts were recorded in a daily journal. Keepers of the Memory have traditionally had an important place in First Nations tradition: they have carried the teachings and understandings to future generations; they have participated in storytelling; they have been called upon to lead in community events.

At this event the Keepers of the Memory included old and young, men and women, from the West Coast to the East, representing many different cultural groups. There could not have been a more representative group of people. They discussed events of the day late into the evening: not only what happened, but the meaning of the events and how best to relate that meaning to their communities.

As the week progressed, the meetings grew later and later, sometimes lasting until two in the morning. Although under enormously heavy schedules, people understood the importance of their work and took very seriously this opportunity to reflect on events of the day. The Keepers of the Memory gave profound insights into the events of the entire convocation.

The most poignant moment of the second convocation for me came following the primate's apology and the subsequent healing service. Mervin Wolfleg of the Siksika First Nation sat in the hushed quiet of the room with his teenaged daughter and her friend beside him as the room emptied all around them. He sat in silence and thoughtfulness for a very long time. With some hesitation I approached him, asking if I could help in any way. With great pain he expressed himself. "The primate is a very good man, a very kind man. I know this and I love him. He is like a father to me. In my culture, in the Siksika Nation, it is wrong to ask a father to apologize. It hurts me very deeply in my heart. It seems to me that we have brought a great shame, a great humiliation upon this man, our primate. I would never ask my own father to apologize. It seems wrong. . . ."

I was astonished at the depth of his love for our primate and at his struggle to reconcile his cultural understanding of apology with the need for his people to move forward in the true freedom and liberation of Christ. Mervin, a profoundly spiritual man, was chosen within his own tradition to be a spiritual leader from the age of six. He spent ten years in residential schools. Mervin suffered from a childhood accident which resulted in a spinal injury. The whippings (with a thick leather belt) he receiving for speaking his own language and for practicing his own culture caused excruciating pain. Yet in this moment, when the apology was delivered, his greatest concern was for the honour of the primate, not for himself. Mervin's willingness to wrestle with painful issues and search for understanding and reconciliation illustrate the commitment of *Dancing the Dream* participants to the healing both of individuals and of communities.

5 / A CALL TO UNITY

We are called to wholeness. We must have balance in our lives and in our persons. We were created to be complete, whole human beings. We have two hands, two eyes, two ears. With our voices, we have to speak with one voice—because if we speak with more than one voice, then we are not speaking the truth.

Our people knew that there would be newcomers coming, and that when they came, they would have spiritual teachings. When our own spiritual teachings were not valued, things were out of balance.

I hold in one hand the understandings of the spiritual tradition in which I was raised, the Siksika Nation. I hold in the other hand the teachings of the Christian religion. I need both to be whole.

I was chosen to be a spiritual leader when I was very young, about six; it was a part of my tradition. Then, I went to residential school and wasn't allowed to practice my religion. It was as though one hand was tied behind my back. I was taught only the Christian way and it was very difficult.

When I finished residential school, I had to learn again how to use my other hand—the hand that held the teachings of my own people. We have to hold our two hands together; both need to be free to work. If we have only one hand, we are not complete.

In my tradition, when we keep our hands together as in prayer, we are saying, "I am going to listen."

Mervin Wolfleg
(Siksika Nation)

Following opening ceremonies, the Most Reverend Michael Peers began the Second National Native Convocation with a reflection on the words of Christ: "Hear, Oh Israel, the Lord our God is one." The primate's message, one of unity and oneness, set the tone for the event.

HEAR, O ISRAEL
Reflection by Michael Peers

The first prayer that Jesus, like all Jewish people, prayed at the beginning of every day was "Hear, O Israel, the Lord our God, the Lord is one."

God is one in life and purpose. Everything God intends is "one." If we look at God's creation, all of creation, all of us are all the work of our Lord and Creator. Creation and the whole universe are one.

Creation has its order. Every part of creation has a place, and there are millions of different aspects of creation. Rocks, waters, human beings—all are the handiwork of one creator: the Lord our God, the Lord is one.

Twenty years ago I was teaching a school for leaders, for future priests of the diocese of Keewatin. We had been talking about whether God's redeeming power was only for human beings or for all creation. One evening, on the edge of the water we saw a beaver. One of the people called the beaver—and the beaver came up on the shore and stood beside us.

The created order is one. The purpose of creation is to live and work and function as one because we are the work of one creator. I never reflect on that truth without seeing that surely with all our diverseness and richness the work of God is one.

But it does not always look like that. The purpose of God has not worked out that way. There is disunion which has entered; and sometimes the parts work against each other, especially with the intervention of human beings.

The Lord our God, the Lord is one. The abuse which the church suffers, the abuse which many suffer, is part of this disunion. We live in a world which needs to be made one and healed—which needs to be made one. For me, one of the great stories of the Gospels is the story of the man brought to Jesus possessed. He was brought to Jesus to be healed and to be made whole.

Jesus asked, "What is your name?" and he replied, "My name is many." He was speaking of what happens when there is division and disunity. It becomes part even of our own souls. What he was saying was, "I am torn apart within myself." His name was "multitude." Jesus healed him so he would be one—one whole person. That healing was a difficult thing. There was a tremendous upheaval within the person and around him. The symbol of the upheaval was that when he became whole, all the powers went somewhere else. To be healed, to be made one, is not easy.

But it is the purpose of Jesus Christ coming into this world. The work of God was to bring healing and restoration to all so that we could share in a world which displays so many signs of brokenness.

It is not simple. We have to learn from the life and death of Jesus. It is costly. His life was taken unjustly, but God holds that society and every society in the full hope of healing and blessing. Jesus rose and is alive. And his resurrection was not simply a demonstration that God cannot be defeated. The resurrection is a sign that *whatever* is broken, destroyed, or dead—including our relationships with ourselves, with one another, with all creation, and with God—can be healed and raised into new life. The resurrection is about all (or the many) becoming one.

One of the great signs in scripture is of the power of tongues. One of the great stories of the Bible is in Genesis. The tower of Babel was one of the lessons to the people. They were trying through their own power to reach heaven and build a tower greater than anything ever seen before. But it was not in harmony with the rest of creation and not built to serve but to boast; and it ended in bitterness, the tower of Babel. People began to speak languages which others could not understand but which existed for their own ends—one of the great signs of disunity and division.

We cannot live in this country without knowing what language and division mean when they come together. The first and most powerful incident in the life of the church was in the story of Pentecost. Most people think here of the "tongues of fire." The greater reality is that the power, the coming of God the Spirit, enabled people to speak and to be understood—people who couldn't otherwise have been understood. The costly work of the Spirit is the undoing of the disunity in our lives and the work of building wholeness, including the capacity to speak and be understood, so that that which has been divided, God unites.

Left to our own devices we can stay in Babel. The spirit of God calls us into a single purpose. God, the Creator, is of a world rich and diverse but with a single purpose. The life of Christ brings wholeness when we are divided within our communities and within our lives.

The Holy Spirit empowers us to speak and to be understood: Hear, O Israel, the Lord our God, the Lord is one.

This call to unity, the affirmation of rich and diverse cultures, led to a convocation that, in the words of Laverne Jacobs, "will be remembered for the pain that was shared, the indomitable strength and faith of a people, the involvement of youth, the generosity and willingness to forgive, and the powerful presence of God's Spirit at work in the gathering."

6 / RESIDENTIAL SCHOOL EXPERIENCES

Almighty Creator,
thank you for coming in the person of our Saviour Jesus Christ,
for the privilege to call you Father.

Our Father, Son, and Holy Spirit,
we come before you this day
and ask your blessing upon all people gathered here;
we pray for those who experienced residential schools.
We pray that you will teach us how to forgive
and to look not only at the bad, but the good things we learned.

We pray for the non-Native people that they will understand
that the hurts have to be brought out
so that the healing can begin.

Thank you for having blessed your people
throughout all the years—
and for this day.

Through Jesus Christ our Lord,
guide us and strengthen us.

    Margaret Waterchief
    (Siksika Nation)

ollowing the primate's *Call to Unity* at the beginning of the second convocation, Margaret Waterchief, a survivor of residential schools and now an ordained priest serving in the Diocese of Calgary, opened the way for sharing the depth of pain within the community with the above prayer. Following her prayer, Mervin Wolfleg sang a song for the healing of the Indian spirit. Mervin explained, "The eagle is a symbol of healing. I sing a song for the healing of the Indian spirit; the song is an acknowledgement of presence of the Creator in creation."

Search For Healing, an award-winning documentary produced by Anglican Video, was shown to delegates, many of whom had attended residential schools. In portraying the experiences of some residential school survivors, the video accurately documented government and church policies that sought to remove indigenous language and culture. As the video ended, some viewers were in shock; some were disoriented; many were angry. Members of the gathered group attempted to comfort each other.

When the planners attempted to move back to the schedule for the day, the group members responded with anger. They wished to continue sharing; and they requested a way to direct their experience, their anger, and their grief to representatives of the church.

After consulting with the planners, Laverne Jacobs called the group together, apologized for "breaking the circle," and invited Michael Peers and his special assistants—Residential Schools Working Unit staff Shirley Harding and John Bird—to the front to listen as members of the formal structure of the Anglican Church of Canada.

In this critical moment, Laverne called on Dominic Eshkakagon. Dominic, a Roman Catholic deacon and respected Ojibwe teacher, served as Elder throughout the convocation. In traditional Aboriginal society, Elders had a special role of guiding the spiritual needs of any group in which they were involved. The role of Elder is reserved for those who have demonstrated integrity in their lives and whose work is guided by compassion. Throughout the eight-day event, in difficult moments, Dominic stepped in with a word of encouragement or with a suggestion for intervention. By the end of the week, all participants had formed a deep respect for Dominic. The youth were particularly fond of him and honoured him with a speech and special gifts.

Dominic had a special role to play as participants began to

deal with residential school abuses. He described his own residential school experience and his journey into healing. He encouraged others to share their pain so that the healing in their own lives could begin.

WE MUST HELP EACH OTHER
by Dominic Eshkakagon

I was in a Catholic residential school. As I listen to my brothers and sisters here, I feel the pain again that I've felt in my own life. I kept the pain inside myself for forty years. I mourn for the little boy whose life ended at the age of nine in 1940 and who didn't begin to live again until 1980. My healing began in 1977 at the death of my father.

On Easter Sunday 1977 six of my eight brothers and sisters were gathered at the home of my parents. My father didn't go to residential school. I remember some of the things I did with my dad, the things he taught me. I remember most of all how he taught me to survive in the bush. When I was eight, the relationship I had with my father died.

I always blamed my father for taking me to the residential school. My mother stayed home with my younger brothers and sisters. I was the oldest. I blamed my dad for what happened at the school because he took me.

I thank the people who hugged me this morning, who gave me the hugs I didn't receive as a child. I went through life without hugs. My mother had been in residential school and didn't know how to parent.

I didn't have parenting skills either. I began to go through a healing process when I lost my son in 1983. I didn't know how to be a father. I didn't know how to listen. I didn't know how to help my son. He took his own life, and he took the life of his own son and his son's mother. This has been a lot of pain for me to live with.

After my Dad died, I don't know how many times I said to my mother, "Mom, I wish I'd shaken Dad's hand when he offered it to me before he died." I wish I'd been able to make amends with him. I'm sorry for what happened. I wish I could now accept his handshake instead of making a sarcastic remark like I did on Easter Sunday. I wish I could say, "Dad, I forgive you." When I could forgive, the little boy in me began to live again; but it was a lost life.

I didn't know how to love. Love was just a word, a substitute for what I now know to be love. I began slowly to learn the process of healing. I was looking after 300 children from my reserve as a counsellor. I was trained as a counsellor, and yet I felt very inadequate to help the students because I didn't know how to help myself. I turned back to the church after my dad's death. I had walked out of the church, lived a life of alcoholism, and even tried to commit suicide.

I woke up one morning, drunk for so long that I couldn't even remember how long. When I got up, there was nobody in the house. My wife was gone; my children were gone; and I began to think to myself, "I'm going to look for my family."

I got into my car. It was hardly running: I drank so much I couldn't afford a good car. I never made any money because I kept spending it back at the bar.

When I got in the car, I said to myself, "Maybe I should drive around until I find them." As I got to the top of a hill, I was feeling very lonely. If I hit the intersection and bank of the river, there would be no trace of me. I started driving as fast as I could.

At the bottom of the hill, I heard a voice calling, "Dad! Dad!" I stopped. I didn't want to take my children with me. When I heard the voice, I thought one of them was in the car.

Today I realize that the things that happened between 1977 and 1983 all had a purpose. I now dedicate my life to helping people who are in pain. I teach people who approach me that God has given us certain gifts to deal with pain and anger and grief. I have learned how to cry. I'm not afraid to cry anymore. One of the people who helped me said one day, "It takes a hell of a good man to be able to cry."

God gave us the gift of anger to express it. Now, when people come to me in grief and in anger, I have a little cushion that I give to them. I say, "Strike out at what gives you anger."

I was struck very hard by a priest when I was just a little boy in residential school. I was molested by the older boys in the school when I was only nine years old.

We need a healing process. We need to share. Not everyone is able to go through the healing process alone. We need someone to help, to teach us how to listen, to be compassionate. We need to learn to listen to and help our brothers and sisters.

We might not be able to wipe away the pain. I still grieve for the little nine-year-old boy whose life ended. I didn't feel freedom in my life. I didn't know how to raise my own children. I didn't know how to respond to my son a few days before he died. I closed my ears to him because I didn't know how to talk to him.

The voice of my son still rings in my ears: "Dad, I need to talk to you. Dad, please talk to me." What hurts the most is that I didn't know how to talk to my son because I didn't know how to be a parent.

Today, I hope that I can help others go through the healing process and be able to forgive.

Dominic began his own sharing on Wednesday morning. Others took up where he left off; and the sharing continued all through Wednesday, all through Thursday, and on into Friday morning. Dozens of people went one by one to the microphone. Some had lost language and culture; some had been abused physically, sexually, or emotionally. Like Dominic, many live with the awareness that they themselves have not known how to parent; cycles of abuse continue in their own communities. Comments by participants during the day included:

We have been carrying the pain all these years; we need to be free people.

It has been hard. At one point this afternoon, I wanted to go away and have a good cry. I've always been of the opinion that there's good and bad [in] what we got out of residential schools. There were some really good Christian people who did their best.

Something I probably never thought about was sexual abuse. Young boys committed suicide because they couldn't live with what happened to them. I think I knew, but it was too horrible to think about. Although I'm concerned about those who worked in the schools and really did try to do their best, it is even more important to help those who are suffering.

When a person sees her own child sexually abused and taking his own life, forgiveness is not simple. But it's the beginning of healing.

Being in residential schools affects everything in us; today it is still hard for me, knowing this is true.

It's good for the leaders to be here, especially the primate, to hear the abuses right from the people.

It's going to take a few more years for forgiveness to happen. The Elders must listen well, with respect. But we have to pray about it, because if we pray for anyone, I know it works.

Speak the truth, and bring hope and peace to others.

Only a few of the many stories shared at the consultation are included here. They begin with those of Eva Louttit, a second-generation residential school survivor; Fred Wale, a man who has spent many years of his life attempting to assist others in education; and Hope Elizabeth Johns, a social worker who has lost two children to suicide.

HOW COULD MY PARENTS LET ME GO?
by Eva Louttit

My parents live in Moose Factory. I went to two residential schools for two years altogether. For the longest time I've felt I was lucky to have come out of that experience intact. This last year I began to really understand that a lot of the hurt and pain were still with me; and in order to heal, I had to deal with them.

When I came into the room this afternoon, I didn't think that I would be able to stand up and talk about my experience. Hearing the pain and hurt shared by others has given me the courage to talk about it. It is especially difficult because my father is in the audience. He went to residential school, and this is the first time that he is going to hear about my experience.

You might think that two years is not very long. I didn't see or experience sexual or physical abuse, but I did experience a lot of psychological abuse. I don't think it is any less devastating to experience psychological and emotional abuse than it is to experience physical and sexual abuse. I remember thinking when I went away, "How can my father let me go? How can my parents let me go knowing what I was going to have to deal with?" Then, as I became older and thought back on it in later years, I realized my parents had no choice. They had to let me go, and I don't feel any bitterness about it now.

I love my parents very much. When I think back to other people who went to residential school with me, I know that we never talked about it with our parents. Once I asked my mother, "How did you feel when I had to go away?" I hadn't seen her cry when we left. I used to think it didn't bother her. My mother said, "I cried after the plane left." She wouldn't cry in front of us—but she cried after the plane left.

I went to Moose Factory to residential school. One of the first things I could remember was having our hair cut. There was a chair in the middle of the room. One by one we came to sit down and have our hair cut off. I looked down and I saw all that black hair around the chair: there were other girls ahead of me, and many of us had long black hair. As I look back on this, it seems to me that it was the first thing that they did to us to try to cut us off from our "Indianness."

The next year I went away to another residential school. Since I was one of the youngest children, they put me in the junior dorm. I had a cousin in the senior dorm, but I never saw her because we weren't allowed to go to another floor.

There were two girls in another dorm who used to run away all the time. I never had the courage to run away. When I was small, I was taught always to listen so I never ran away even though I would have liked to. Every time those two girls who ran were caught, they were brought back to the school and all the junior girls were gathered up. We were lined up along the beds. They brought the girls in, pulled their pants down in front of all of us, and made us look, even if we didn't want to look. They strapped the two girls with a strap. I remember thinking I didn't want to look (I knew what they were feeling, the shame and the humiliation), but we had to look. This happened quite a few times. They would run away and be strapped in front of us.

We were always lining up to go here and there. Everywhere. This was such a totally different life from what I was used to. I came from a loving home, a closely knit family and an extended family. It was so strange to live like that, because it wasn't like that in my own home.

I don't remember much of what we had to eat, but I remember that on Friday nights we used to get fish. I felt that what we had was never enough because I was never full. On Fridays when we had fish, I would get two or three and finish them off really quickly because I liked them. I used to think, "I wish I had more," but I never had more.

Nights were the worst time because we were alone with our thoughts. It was at night when we thought of our families that we had left behind. We thought of the love and security that were there. I grew up not really knowing my brothers and sisters because when I was at home, the older ones were gone, and then I left home and didn't know the younger ones.

When my own daughter was three or four years old and woke up in the night, I found an anger coming out when I was with her. I don't know if she remembers, and it only lasted a few months; but when I think of the psychological damage I could have done, I don't know if I can ever forgive myself for doing that to my own child. I began to realize what I was doing, though, and made a conscious effort to stop. I have never had the courage to talk about this with my daughter yet.

When I think back on the way I used to do things and the way I still do things, I wonder if it was because of what I went through at residential school. I learned to build a wall around myself. I learned not to let people see the real me. I had to get to know people for a long time before I could really let people get to know who I really was, let my own person come out. I still do that to this day. I've been called quiet and timid because I won't let people see who I really am.

I went to high school away from home as well, staying in foster homes in the south. When I finished, I had to go back and listen to my aunts and uncles telling stories to help me get back my own culture. When I went back up north to work, people would call me "white man" because I had lost so much over the years I was away. They called me "white man" because I had acquired so many of the white ways.

I lost a lot of my own culture, and I knew that the only way that I could get it back was to go back up north. Then my own people called me "white man" because that was the way that I acted.

It took me a long time to learn again about my own culture and my own language. I didn't lose my own language entirely. We weren't allowed to speak our own language in school; but when the supervisor wasn't looking, we would sneak away and talk in our own language. I lost a lot which I had to gain back when I went back north. To this day I speak the language, but I don't speak it very well. Sometimes when I hear the Elders speak, there are a lot of words that I don't understand; that causes me a lot of pain. There are parts of my own culture that I know that I'll never get back.

It's very difficult for me to face this day because I knew the hurt and the pain and the tears would be there, but I knew I had to face it because it's a part of my healing. I knew I had to become whole again, and I believe that God brought me here to be a part of all this.

This is God's way: to bring me to a place where I could start to deal with this—and so I can continue on. I'm really thankful that I'm in a place where I can tell my story and be comfortable enough with the people I'm with to tell that story. I have hope that I will be able to continue to talk about and deal with it until I can put it in its proper perspective.

WE HURT INSIDE
by Fred Wale

I never expected to be up here, to be listening to the people who had experiences at residential school. I experienced the same things, the same hardships.

This morning I couldn't even talk after the residential school film. I broke down. It just brought back so many memories I've never talked about. I've never discussed the residential experience with my parents, with my sisters, with my friends. This is the first time.

Why? Because I think that so many of the people who spent time in the schools were hurt. They were hurt inside; and when you hurt inside, it's pretty hard to leave it behind. We didn't have counselling. We didn't have people to come and hug us when we needed it. I know I needed hugging at times. I was only seven or eight years old when I went.

I used to get slapped by a supervisor. I remember one time: one of my buddies was caught talking to one of his sisters. The supervisor put a pack on his back and made him run twenty times around the yard. Is that education?

My late parents were very humble people. They raised thirteen of us at a time when there was no family allowance and no welfare. They figured that at residential school we would be well educated. We weren't well educated. I picked up my English on the streets after I left residential school.

It was very hard to do that. I made it up to Grade 10, but my writing is like shorthand. I can't spell, and I really can't read my own writing myself. In my time at residential school, we only spent two hours in the classroom each day. The federal government placed us there and believed that they were doing a good deed for Native people; but we were working a lot of the time.

I used to get thrown out of bed at five in the morning to milk five cows. That was my education. Just when I left the residential school, milking machines were invented.

I worked at B.C. Hydro for a number of years. Then there was an opportunity for a job at the Department of Indian Affairs for home school counsellors. I asked my father's advice about it. My father encouraged me to take the job. He said, "Money is not everything,

Freddie. Our Native people have been fenced in. We have so many stumbling blocks to overcome." If any of us wanted to borrow money to start a business, we wouldn't be able to go to a bank if we lived on a reserve. There are many, many stumbling blocks that we have had as Native people.

I was struggling to make a decision about whether to leave a good job at B.C. Hydro or to go to work counselling students. It was a tough decision because I had four young kids. At that time I began to realize what my own parents went through in raising thirteen children.

My father said, "Money is not everything, sonny. Take that position. You might not make much, but at least you will be working with your own people." I worked with Native people in our own area for fourteen years. My salary wasn't good, and I travelled through many communities to visit the students where they were studying.

When I now listen to people who are crying, I'm with you. I don't know how we are going to get away from all the hurt that is inside us.

I knew about some of the sexual abuses that were happening in residential school, but we couldn't help because we were not free to speak. If you told on someone, you got punished.

I still have scars on the inside of my lips from when I got hit across the face with a key chain. That scar would never go away. The scars on my heart will never go away. My wife attended residential school. There are times that I would have liked to have talked about it, but I never got a response from her.

Why? I think we've heard the reasons why. People are hurt inside and it's hard to talk about. My father and mother were very religious people. I believe the reason I can speak English and read is because I attended church regularly. The federal government system of Indian education did not work for Native people.

We're crying for help. I'm glad that this opportunity for talking came about. In the video, there was anger for me. I just wanted to get up right away. I was in tears. I was speechless.

I encouraged my kids to attend school, to finish high school. My oldest one is now teaching; my second one is in third year at the University of British Columbia; my third child is a journeyman carpenter; and my youngest hasn't made a decision yet about her future. I have six grandchildren now.

My kids say that I spoiled them when I heard them crying—but I haven't told them the things that happened to me. The reason that I have spoiled my kids is because their cry hurt me inside.

I thank God for giving me this time to say a few words. May God bless you people.

I'VE LEFT THE ANGLICAN CHURCH
by Elizabeth Hope Johns

I am from the Nlha'7 kapmx Nation from Lytton, B.C. I was a student at St. George's Anglican Residential School for ten years. I entered when I was six. I vividly remember that day. My mother left me, and I never saw her again for quite a few years. I don't remember the next four years. That time is like a black spot. I remember only a few things.

One memory was being in a group of little girls squatting in a huddle like little chicks trying to keep each other warm because we weren't let in. We were locked out. We were supposed to run around, to stretch our legs, but it was really cold. Our dresses were thin— and we were thin. Some of the girls were so cold they were crying. They just couldn't get warm.

Another memory is of a little girl who couldn't speak English and didn't know how to ask for the bathroom. She was looking around for a bathroom; and finally when she couldn't hold it any longer, she went to the bathroom beside a lilac bush and was beaten for that. The bathrooms they had for us were really scary. The water was continually running; and no one took the time to explain the bathroom to us: how it was different than what we were used to and how it worked.

When I was about ten or so, my grandparents took me home at Christmas and during the summer holidays. I learned the language, culture, spirituality, and traditional ways.

I was married when I was quite young to an alcoholic and abusive husband. I left him after eight years when I had five children. When I was a single parent, my own mother used to come to help me. While I was cooking and cleaning, she played with the children. She was really giving: she hugged and kissed us and we really enjoyed this. It was like a gift to us; it was just what we needed. She had gone to residential school as a child for six years as well.

During residential school days, the same things happened to me as to many others here. I couldn't use my own language, but I didn't know my language as well as others. In school those who spoke their own language were punished. They were slapped across the face. I felt sorry for them then, and I still do because of the pain that they carry.

When I was about thirteen, I got slapped across the face by the administrator. I thought my head was going to come off. His finger-prints were left on my face, and he wouldn't allow me to go to school for a few days. It happened during choir practice. I was counting the little squares up on the ceiling. My punishment for not singing was that I was slapped across the face. I was slapped across the face again when I moved into another dorm. Somehow a young man had managed to enter the dorm. I didn't even know he was there, but I was blamed for it and punished for something that I hadn't done.

I never knew violence until I went to residential school where I saw a lot of it. There were about 100 girls and 100 boys. I remember once a girl died in the infirmary. She had been sick and was taken to the infirmary. We heard that she wasn't taken to the hospital soon enough and that was why she died. We were very scared by this, and we all tried not get sick.

Being a parent now, I feel it was wrong to just leave children at a residential school without preparing them. People should have told us how many years we were to be there and why we were there—to learn to read and write. I remember one elderly teacher there. I re-member that she hugged me. She probably hugged others. I re-member her well.

I worked for the residential school later, and my own children were admitted to the same school. The residential school closed in 1979. My boys disclosed in the mid-eighties that they had been sexually abused by a child care worker in the seventies. Many inter-mediate boys ages nine to fourteen had been sexually abused. One week before my oldest son was to testify at the trial of the child care worker, he committed suicide. One and a half years later my second son committed suicide. Of the young boys who disclosed sexual abuse, only a handful are now left. Many have committed suicide.

I went through a lot of therapy, and I'm still going to therapy. Af-ter my second son passed away, I didn't know what to do with my-self. I wanted to commit suicide myself. I blamed myself. I still do. I blamed the church for the longest time. I now understand it wasn't the church itself but the people who worked for the church who were abusive. They punished children for speaking their own lan-guage and for not understanding another culture. I changed my faith and went to the Bahai religion. I found it closer to my own culture and my own spirituality.

After nine months of therapy, my community nudged me and said, "Do something else. Find a way to get an education and to help the people who are hurting as you have been hurt." This is what I'm doing now. I have completed my third year of social work at the University of Victoria. I have struggled with the courses at times, and I've been tempted to quit; but my classmates have told me, "The more you learn, the more you give." I have felt encouraged to carry on, and I now have one more year to complete.

Life is very precious. I am now doing my second practicum in a crisis centre in my own community. The suicide rate is dropping. We are talking about abuse more openly. We are able to get things out in the open. There are lots more resource people. We encourage everyone to ask for help. Even though things are much more in the open, it is still difficult for some to talk—to share their abuse and hurt.

I am grateful to the Anglican Church for the funding from the Residential Schools Working Group which has helped to bring healing to our community.

Mervin Wolfleg, a member of the Siksika Nation (Blackfoot) near Calgary, worked for twelve years with the Indian Association of Alberta as a cultural development worker and manager of youth services. He has worked as a consultant to his band on organizational and personnel development. In this process he developed a strategy for changing the government structure of his band to make it more suitable to their own cultural traditions. He has worked for three and one-half years in the United States in a cross-cultural program called the North American Cultural Appreciation Team. He trained alcohol and drug counsellors through the Nechi Institute on Alcohol and Drug Education. He has volunteered for twenty years in alcohol and drug counselling within his community. After graduating from the University of Calgary with a bachelor of education with distinction in 1986, he worked in the Siksika Nation schools for seven years. During that time his main work was as director of Student Services for six years and in liaison and consultation with three counties and the Siksika Nation in a total of thirteen schools.

A SONG FOR HEALING
by Mervin Wolfleg

Different tribes have been separated, and we are now to be reconciled as brothers and sisters in spite of our tribal differences and divisions. We are one in faith and baptism. We are one body under the chieftainship of Jesus Christ. We are called to be pilgrims on a pilgrimage. We are called to follow by faith and belief. Our forefathers and foremothers were called to trust and be obedient to God.

It took me thirty years to talk about what began to happen forty years ago when I went to residential school. I only knew my younger brother. It was a sin to look at someone else. I couldn't even look at my sister. The priest you saw in that film: the priest was married and [we believed] having an affair with our teacher. . . . That was my introduction to the holy house.

We saw the video. My older brother was in the video. He has a lot of anger. He was also in the residential school. He has been kicked out of two counties. If white people talked to him in any kind of a demeaning way, he'd lash out. This happened even at football games in Calgary when he was in high school. This is the kind of anger that has existed in the Blackfoot community.

I have seven children and I have raised nine foster children, most in a Traditional way. I lost one in a car accident. Children are my best friends; I'm living my childhood through my children. The hurt of residential schools is a hurt that is going to go on through two or three generations.

I went through learning in the Traditional way and had a vision quest. My grandmother was my guide. Through that spirituality I have learned, so I have come here.

My observation is that when the money went, the residential schools closed and the church left our communities. That is why we are so poor on our reserves, in our churches. The church has to look at how the church is now operating on the reserves. The damage was done; and now we, as Aboriginal ministers, have to do the repairing and the healing, but we have been abandoned again.

Traditional ways are dying off. Missionaries did a good job of discouraging Traditional ways. A lot of us carry our own spirituality. I survived through to my teenage years with my own Traditional ways through God-gifted people.

The churches have a lot of wisdom they need to share. My children have a lot of wisdom, and we need to hear it. If a young child can pray, that prayer is the most powerful prayer that you can get.

I'm still going through healing. It's very easy for me to be turned off, to shut off the English language. I was punished for speaking my own language. I had a spinal injury before I went to school. At residential school they strapped me on my bare bottom for every time I was caught speaking my own language. That's why it's hard for me to speak in English today. We are struggling with the larger church and with the larger culture, trying to express ourselves.

It is hard for me to communicate with you in this kind of a setting with stuffed animals, my own brothers and sisters, all around. They were stuffed because animals are not respected by others as they are by us. We've lost our spirituality when we come to a place like this. There is a lot of hurt, a lot of pain. My children are helping me with this.

I still do sweats. I still do the medicine pipe ceremony. I still dance, sing, and speak my own language. This is our gift.

We ask our children to be with us, but I'm scared because I don't trust white people. I am afraid they will take my message and judge it by their culture and by their language. It will then come back to us as Indian people, and it won't be the same. The dialogue has to continue and we have to be part of it.

The primate has said that he will take the dialogue to places where we can't go; and I say, "Well, why can't we go?"

Annie Buck, youth delegate from Moose Lake, Manitoba, shared the ongoing struggle of many among the youth. She spoke on behalf of many youth whose lives continue to be marked by abuse long after the closing of the residential schools. The painful reality is that abuses didn't stop with the closing of the schools.

PLEASE LISTEN: A PLEA FROM THE YOUTH
by Annie Buck

I stand here as a young person because today we need to have young people speaking for themselves.

My experiences won't compare to the residential school experiences, but I have had the sexual abuse you are talking about. When I was a little girl, the abuses began.

I have found it in my heart to forgive. Today young people are afraid. What has happened in the past still happens. Young people are still being hurt.

We want you to listen to us; we have a lot to talk about. The scars we have today are for the pain that happened in our families and in residential schools. We have those scars on our bodies.

I have found it hard to open up and tell the story of what I went through. I thank God there was this person, a priest, who was very helpful. My healing began when I understood [the priest] wanted to listen. I thought I was alone; nobody wanted to listen to me. I wondered, "Why? Is it because I don't know anything?"

We are young. We go through a lot of pain, including alcohol and addictions. Life has been rough sometimes. I need the experience of hearing others tell their stories, the problems they face, how they deal with their problems. You have to open yourselves up, to be there to support and to listen to us. The main thing is that you show that you care, that you love young people. I knew my priest loved me and cared for me; she was there to listen.

We can't seem to open up because we're afraid inside. I never told anyone what I went through. I thought of myself as a slave. . .

I know there are still trials ahead, trials that we face in the world. I have a grandpa who told me he loved me. He told me he loved me and to try to live right for God. I never used to listen, because I was stubborn. Often it's when we lose a loved one that we know we have to change. We can't wait until we lose a loved one. We have to change now. I thank God for being here, that I have the courage to stand and to share.

We are the future; therefore we are given ears to listen to what our people went through in the past. All of us have our own stories.

The search for healing is often a long journey to wholeness which includes great spiritual growth. Abuse victims often blame themselves. The abuse affects their self-esteem. In the final sharing of this chapter, Andrew Wesley, a community leader who is working to bring healing to youth in his own community, outlines the need for resources for spiritual healing from abuse.

NEVER BE AFRAID
by Andrew Wesley

My uncle once said, "Never be afraid; never be scared; never run away." It is important to challenge. The church has to do something so the youth can come back to the church, so they can know who they are. We are dealing with human beings. The statistics of our youth show that there are so many suicides.

We have the opportunity with the church to work in a constructive way. We have to make [the church] understand that we are dealing with human beings, with souls that are lost. We have to bring them back to the church.

Last week we had a reunion of people who had been to residential school. I was on a panel. We heard the testimony of those who had been sexually abused. A child who had been abused in residential school asked me, "Is the brother who abused me going to heaven?" I didn't know what to say. The boy said, "If he's going to heaven, I don't want to go to heaven."

Of thirty children I know in my own community who were abused, four committed suicide; six still consider themselves dirty; four were healed through Traditional healing.

There are times we have to challenge the church when we see an injustice is done. I believe we are allowed by our God, by our maker, to challenge injustice. I challenge the church to do something for our young people. We have to do something for our young people.

Our young people are lost; they are looking for their identity. We have to do something for the youth who have been abused so they can come back to the church, so they can become healed, so they can know who they are.

An apology is not enough. We need programs for healing because the government won't provide funds for religious or spiritual healing. And this spiritual healing is what our children need. We are dealing with their souls.

RESPONSES AND REACTIONS

An elder
Listen, hear, and believe what young people say when they come to you. Be grandmothers and grandfathers to these people, and be open.

Dominic Eshkakagon

Participants
We couldn't say anything, so we said a prayer in our small group. It was after the prayer that people started to talk. I was really moved by that. It's so wonderful, that God is at work here.

Pain and suffering have to be talked about, but it is like opening up a wound. What are we going to do for people when they go home?

A prayer
Thank you, holy Father, for this gathering and for my own personal healing. The way to be healed is in this way:
we become aware of our problems;
we talk about problems to someone—a priest or a counsellor;
we give away the secrecy of the problem which is giving us pain;
we shed tears that open our hearts for healing;
we let go and let God.

Louisa Roberts

7 / ABORIGINAL AND CHRISTIAN

The Second National Native Convocation had a number of ecumenical and international guests who brought warm messages of hope and solidarity. Throughout the world members of an international network of Indigenous peoples are increasingly discovering links among their cultures. Indigenous cultures globally are rich and varied; all have a similar and deep respect for all of creation. From the Maori cultures of New Zealand to the cultures of Africa, the experience of church has many parallels. Indigenous peoples have often found their own cultures to be marginalized, and they have had similar struggles to reclaim their own cultures and heritages and to bring their own gifts to the larger church community nationally and internationally.

This chapter includes reflections by several of the ecumenical and international guests at the convocation. Stan McKay, a former moderator of the United Church of Canada, offers insights from his own experience. The Right Reverend Whakahuihui Vercoe, Te Pihopatanga O Aotearoa (Bishopric of Aotearoa), New Zealand, shares the journey of Maori people to worship in ways which reflect their own cultural heritage. James Isbister provides an example of the painful separations which now exist in many Aboriginal communities. The chapter concludes with a vision of a Native church by a Roman Catholic ecumenical partner who also served as Elder, Dominic Eshkakagon.

Stan McKay was born in 1942 in Fisher River, Manitoba. The youngest of a family of five, Stan grew up in a relatively isolated Cree community with few links to the outside world. His parents lived a traditional Aboriginal lifestyle. His father provided a living for his family through traditional fishing and trapping; Stan's mother cared for the family in the absence of his father. The young family was supported by Elders, grandparents, and a larger community which had its own integrity and autonomy.

Aware of the massive social changes occurring in the wider world, Stan's family encouraged the children to get an education. Because they lived a traditional lifestyle and had no savings, their only option for educational opportunities was through residential schools. Stan succeeded in the education system but was deeply aware of how culturally different were those who provided "education" in the residential schools. Stan was also profoundly aware of the alienation he felt from home and community while in school.

Influenced by family involvement in the sixties in the Friendship Centre movement, which encouraged hearing the voices of Native peoples, Stan studied education and began a career in teaching before being ordained in the United Church in 1971. He has witnessed massive changes in his own communities as well as those in which he has served. He served the communities of Norway House and Fisher River before becoming national coordinator of Native Ministries in the United Church of Canada in 1981. He became director of the Dr. Jessie Saulteaux Resource Centre, an Aboriginal theological centre, in 1988 and moderator of the United Church of Canada from 1992 to 1994. Stan currently serves with the World Council of Churches Committee on Justice, Peace and the Integrity of Creation.

A REFLECTION ON BEING ABORIGINAL AND CHRISTIAN
The Right Reverend Stan McKay

People of many nations, sisters and brothers: It has been an honour for Dorothy and me to spend time together with you. I bring greetings from the United Church of Canada.

Over the week I have come to respect your process here. Many people are working very hard and with late hours to keep this process in place. It's good to have met your primate again.

I appreciated the morning prayer with words, "You call us to be whole." It has focused right on the issue which is central to this gathering: to be Aboriginal and Christian. I have struggled to understand what it means to be Aboriginal, to have a culture which is rich and unique.

It is interesting that the church has been able to acknowledge the rich and diverse cultures within the global context for the last twenty years. People have been saying it is good in Africa and other parts of the world to acknowledge cultures there as special. The resolve of the church not to acknowledge my own people has continued to be painful for me. I, too, am a survivor of five years in residential school. I, too, have been an "object" of mission. I have dealt throughout my twenty-two-year ministry with a deep anger which has sometimes surfaced. In the local context, the residential schools were established because Aboriginal culture was seen as lacking in cultural depth and, in some expressions, was seen as an evil way of life.

The fact that the biblical language could be translated into Cree was a reflection of the richness and the spiritual quality of the philosophy of my people. Because the philosophy is rich, we also had a language which expressed our spiritual understandings.

When the explorers came and asked, "What is this place?" the people responded with the work *khanatum*, which in Cree means "sacred place," holy ground. This is the root of the name Canada. It is not surprising that in Cree we had some trouble understanding what shepherds and sheep were in biblical illustration, living as we did in the muskeg. We were more familiar with muskrats. But our ancestors knew about theological concepts; they had the insight to deal with biblical concepts. How could another culture see us as pagan, as poor children? Our ancestors had a sense of the sacredness of all life.

We have known God long before the missionaries came. We are First Nations people. We have gifts to share with the wider church. We are "Keepers of the Earth." Let us acknowledge the sacredness of our connectedness to the earth and to all of creation.

The results of historical misunderstanding have meant that there has been cultural oppression, of which the churches have had a part. How do we deal with what has happened to us? Some say forgive, but what about those whose lives are still affected by the cycles of destruction? Let us acknowledge what has happened and be about the business of healing.

I went to the first meeting dealing with residential schools in your church some years ago. There was a deep sense of the correctness of this process being not just about residential schools but for healing in Aboriginal society. It is also about the staff and others in the system of the residential schools. While we are victims, we have an ability to respond. We can take initiative in healing. Healing isn't done *for*, it is done *with*. In most situations of abuse and healing, one can involve all participants in the healing process.

The convocation is in part a naming of our and the churches' involvement in an oppressive and abusive relationship. In our deep respect and humility, we have been taken advantage of by the dominant culture; but in some ways we allowed it to happen. This is not only about healing for ourselves; it is for the whole of society. Racism is real and powerful, and it continues to erode the self-esteem of Aboriginals as a people.

I go to Native Traditional ceremonies. I need healing also in a nonjudgemental way, a way which is affirming. In our healing circles the call is to action. There is pain. We are not to blame, but we are to deal with the shame and self-hate which we have felt.

My feeling is that the whole society needs to be healed. My sense is that the oppression is carried on in different forms. Institutions carry on the systematic problems of oppression. In the place of residential schools, we now have youth centres and prisons for Aboriginal men and women. Most public schools prolong the suffering because they do not present what really happened historically.

Historically in the church there were crusades. In those crusades people were saying, "Believe like us, or we will cut off your heads." We are calling for liberation from this oppressive image of what it is to be the church.

My Dakota friends could tell you of their experience with the incoming settlers. Their lives were declared invalid. Many lost their lives. This practice of genocide is international. People in different parts of the world have suffered in this way and go on suffering. The historic actions of the church have drawn us into a place where the church acts out of judgement. The loss is that we give up our place as people of spiritual discernment. We must move in solidarity to discernment from judgement. This is a task for many parts of the world.

I invite people to be involved in what I understand to be the central element in our spiritual future: what it is to be *both Aboriginal and Christian.* There have been divisions in our communities so that some in the Traditional way say that you cannot be both Christian and Traditional and some in the Christian church say that you cannot be both Traditional and Christian.

It is my understanding that spirituality is not about a separation, but about a respect that does not limit the spiritual journey. We do have options and choices to make in our spiritual journey. Each of us must respect others who make those choices. It is the young people of our communities who will be making those choices for their generation.

Recently in a United Church gathering, people were saying, "There are young people here, and these young people are the leaders of tomorrow." A young person rose and said, "We are the leaders of today." We have to listen to them because they will bring us healing. They will show us the way to our own healing. They will flee from our churches if we are judgemental and exclusive.

The gospel is communicated at times in a way which is historically incorrect; it lacks some of the spirit of God which calls us into community. We practice our spirituality and our faith in the context of many differences and changes. The gospel describes Samaritans as neighbours. Well, the Anishinabe are neighbours. It is often in biblical story that the dispossessed and marginalized are the ones to whom God comes. Jesus came in the spirit of the law—not to use the law as a weapon.

There was a historical misunderstanding between those who brought the gospel from Europe and those who already lived in this land. In 1986 in the United Church, we received an apology:

Long before my people journeyed to this land, your people were here; and you received from your Elders an understanding of creation, and of the Mystery that surrounds us all, that was deep and rich and to be treasured.

We did not hear you when you shared your vision. In our zeal to tell you of the good news of Jesus Christ, we were blind to the value of your spirituality.

We confused Western ways and culture with the depth and breadth and height of the gospel of Christ.

We imposed our civilization as a condition for accepting the gospel. We tried to make you like us, and in so doing we helped to destroy the vision that made you what you were. As a result you and we are poorer; and the image of the Creator in us is twisted, blurred; and we are not what we are meant by the Great Spirit to be.

We who represent the United Church of Canada ask you to forgive us and to walk together in the spirit of Christ so that our people may be blessed and God's creation may be healed.

When the apology was made, the Elders said, "It is not over." When

It is not over.

we built a stone cairn, the Elders told us not to finish it. We practically completed it; and they said, "The rest will take some time." It therefore is a symbol of the ongoing work that needs to be done to bring about healing.

I have appreciated the quality of sharing that I've experienced at this gathering. This sharing is a model of healing in community. In your gentleness you have revealed the depth of hurt and anger. Anger is something that we must not deny; it is to remind each other of the goodness of God and to make us strong people together. God calls us to wholeness.

I have a dream. The gift of God is that our people, our children, will be healed. I believe the will of God is for all people to live with dignity.

Convocation delegates were helped in understanding the need to affirm the culture and tradition of Aboriginal members of the church by the dynamic Bishop Vercoe and his wife Doris from Aotearoa. Beginning their talk with a song of their people, they shared their journey, indicating the tremendous growth in their own country of Aotearoa (New Zealand), translated as "A Long White Cloud."

A LONG WHITE CLOUD
The Right Reverend Whakahuihui Vercoe

We are a tribal people. Our tribes are strong. We live in a country which is translated to be called "A Long White Cloud." We were discovered by the Dutch; then we were rediscovered by Captain Cook. There are five hundred major tribes in our country and over 5,000 family units. We had many wars but we only fought during daylight hours. We were told this was not right when we were colonized. Eventually we went to war to defend our homes, our mountains, our rivers and seas. Now we are still at war, but we do it through the courts. We do it through the highest legal courts throughout the whole land.

We came here to listen, to observe, to share, and to take back your story. We came not to judge; and we came not to present you with answers, because that is for you to decide. The people of the land in our country are called the "Keepers of the Land." I am grateful to your primate, who was instrumental in inviting us. And so we open with a song: we come with open hands and sing a song of thanksgiving in order that you may take your place among the whole of creation.

This is one of the occasions when we can share who and what we are as children of Jesus Christ. We come and present these things to him as offerings of ourselves. I have listened to the pain and to the history; I will not presume to say that I understand your pain, but I would like to tell you about our church.

Behold, I bring you tidings of great joy.

This was a song of angels on the plains of Bethlehem. This message was brought to our people by the Reverend Mr. Samuel, who was a chaplain. A chief brought this man. After he preached in 1814, people asked, "What is this man speaking about?" He said, "The time will come when you will understand."

There were treaties dealing with our lands, our forests, our seas, our customs, and our religions; and we were to allow our brothers and sisters to settle with us. We went to war when our lands were confiscated, and we were branded rebels. The missionary church had settled in our land. As its members grew, it formed its constitution without Maori involvement.

So in fact, we have had two Anglican churches growing side by side in our country. Maori people asked that the church recognize their sovereignty as keepers of the land, as people in partnership. What happened was that the teachings of the gospel were understood in our own way and in our own time and in our own traditions. We wanted to walk hand in hand and to do it in our own way, and this didn't happen until 1976. Since 1976 the church has grown dramatically.

I believe we had to have our own sense of what needs doing, our own structure, and to do it in our own way. We are growing very swiftly as we do this. My prayer is that you will find your own way, your own faithfulness and your own Nativeness. We believe that this is God's calling and you will succeed.

We give thanksgiving that we were a part of this convocation in the home that you call "holy ground"—Canada. This is your heritage. Claim it. Use it. Make it part of the fabric of your lives with your children in your communities and in your nations.

In response to the talks by Hui Vercoe and by Stan McKay, James Isbister was moved to speak.

It is good to hear from different churches. We Aboriginal people were united people, not divided by churches. It is important to be honest, to begin by defining who we are as Aboriginal people. The Aboriginal people believe this is a sacred land—clear and holy. This is an opportunity now for us to realize another pain that has to be dealt with so we can begin to truly heal as people. I could feel the feelings you have had as our brothers of different countries as you shared with us the "long white cloud." We, too, are a tribal people. Our tribes are strong.

James and many leaders have struggled from an early age to affirm both the stories of an oral literary Tradition and Christian teachings. This struggle continues for many people. From the first day of the convocation, Keepers of the Memory shared moments of deep pain. Some have been excluded from involvement in their band councils because they are Christian and not Traditional; others, who have been recovering their Traditional culture, have been excluded from involvement in the Christian church.

This rift has caused enormous pain. It has created splits in individuals, in families, and in communities. In the past few years, many of the leaders called to be priests who serve in their own communities are attempting to find ways to bring healing. There are times that the divisions between peoples of different denominations are extremely painful.

James, of Plains Cree heritage, is now serving an inner city parish in Prince Albert. He was a school counselor for a number of years and has served in his own community of Ahtahakoop Reserve (Sandy Lake) as well as serving three terms, one as chairperson, on the Council for Native Ministries. Of the division he sees in many communities, he has said, "For the sake of our people, we must find ways to bring healing. We must try to include Aboriginal traditional people because they hold strong cultural values. Since the beginning of my ministry, I have tried to build bridges, to include traditional people, and to show respect to all people regardless of denomination."

James shares an incident that illumines the importance of respecting all community members and that affirms the leadership of traditional Elders.

PAINFUL SEPARATIONS
The Reverend James Isbister

In my community there was a terrible accident in which four people

79

died. Two were from my own community; two, from a neighbouring community. I was involved in the wake services and funerals from my own community. I was asked to go to a wake service in the neighbouring community.

The evening of the wake service, when I arrived at the band hall, things seemed quite disorganized. I was asked to assist in the formal part of bringing the bodies to the front of the hall. I stood at the front and led this.

One of the people killed was Anglican; another was Pentecostal. They were first cousins; their mothers were sisters. There was a group of Pentecostals gathered around the Pentecostal person. They were focusing only on that person. They were ignoring completely the Anglican person. I was very concerned about this kind of separation in my own community.

I have tried to work closely with the Traditional Elders from other communities; we have come to respect each other, and I have been impressed with their integrity. Here, I was again impressed with the integrity of the Traditional Elder.

After some time I was increasingly uncomfortable with the way the people were making a great fuss over one body and ignoring the other. It was the Traditional Elder who went to the family of the Anglican and shook their hands; then he went to the family of the Pentecostal person and shook their hands. After him, one by one, all the members of the community went: some Catholic, some Anglican, some who had gone previously to the Pentecostal, and some who were Traditional. That long line of people led by the traditional Elder affirmed all. They made no divisions, no separations, between denominations.

As I saw this happen—this affirmation of the grief of both families, honouring of the bodies of both—I could not help but think that the community was led in this by the Traditional Elder, by the one who had been despised.

Dominic Eshkakagon was born on Manitoulin Island and moved with his family to Spanish River Indian Reserve, now called Sagamok Anishinabek, when he was a young child. He began training early in Traditional ways; he spent his teenage years working with his grandmother who was a herbalist and a medicine woman. He has worked as a lumberman, construction worker, and truck driver at various times. He began to work for his reserve as a counselor in 1970 and was ordained a deacon in the Roman Catholic Church in 1983. Dominic passed away on October 9, 1994. At the convocation Dominic shared his vision of a Native church.

A VISION OF A NATIVE CHURCH
Elder Dominic Eshkakagon

At the age of nine I was sexually molested by older boys in the residential school I attended. I spent my life searching for love. It wasn't until 1980 that I realized how this had affected my life. When I realized what was happening, I changed—and I've apologized to those I've abused in my life.

There are so many things we need to look at in our lives. Each time we tell a story, we find something new, something we didn't know before. In order to be healed, we have to bring out the hurts and express these things. Let the pain flow from you. It is okay to cry.

I am thankful to you for the hospitality and to the Roman Catholic bishops for making my time here possible. It has been a very good experience to be here. When I report back to my bishops, they're going to hear things they didn't expect to hear. As we went through the pain of our residential school years, I felt the pain again.

I have worked with the Anglican church for many years, sharing ways of Native spirituality. It is commendable that your church leaders are here to listen, to hear you express your pain and anger. I haven't had the opportunity in the Catholic Church to experience that.

I am a deacon. I do most things that priests do. I help in baptism preparation and in baptisms. I help prepare for first communion and confirmations. I perform funerals and weddings. I help the church to bring our Native spirituality back. I don't always agree with everything that happens, but we have to start somewhere.

When we talk about how we can approach the Father, as Native people I see many ways of doing this. As we approach the last part of the creed which says "the holy catholic Church," it still hurts me to know that the translation of *Catholic* means "universal." To me, this means that every culture should be recognized in the world where the church is. The church is not now a universal church. It must become that. It must be part of the culture of all people.

We have been told to "let go of the apron strings and learn to stand on your own two feet." But this has not happened. I look forward to the day when we do let go of the apron strings.

Remember what Jesus said in Matthew's Gospel. He said that he came not to destroy the law or the prophets but to fulfill them. It is my hope that the prophesies of our Native people will be a reality and that we will have a truly universal church.

It is wonderful to see here today our own Native people serving as priests. We do not have this freedom in the Catholic Church. We have only celibate priests. I believe we have only two Native priests on the continent of North America, which we call Turtle Island.

I do purification ceremonies as well as penitential ceremonies. I use the pipe for thanksgiving ceremonies. It's beautiful to be part of these ceremonies. I look forward to the day when we may use the most beautiful prayer of our Tradition, the sunrise ceremony, in the church.

This is the most beautiful prayer because it is a prayer from the heart. As the light of the sun touches each of the elements of the earth, we give thanks for each element that we see. It is beautiful to look up and to see the sun first touch the birds flying high above. We pray as the light touches the tops of the trees and moves down to the lake and rocks, the elements all around us. Our prayers are said in freedom at the beginning of each day—and each day is new. The circumstances of each day are different, so we use a prayer which suits the circumstance.

We give thanks for all. All is given by the Creator. We take the pipe and pray in four directions, offering tobacco to the pipe. We share the pipe with one another. Once we've done that, we take pure, clear water and share that. As each takes water, we give thanks for the gift of the water. Without water, there is no life.

It is my hope that there will be a day when we will be truly a Native church and we will all be children of the Father and we will be the ones to plan our own destiny. We will use all our own prayers to celebrate the eucharist.

I've talked to our own bishops and some Roman Catholic clergy, and I tell them truly that the Native way to pray is what Jesus taught. Jesus taught that whenever two or three are gathered in his name, he is there.

Where I come from, I am also known as a medicine man. I use the medicines of my people to help heal. It is important to discern those who use medicines for good and those who might use them for bad. As I began to understand my own Native spirituality, I began to use more of the positive, incorporating those in my Christianity.

I was born a First Nations person; I was baptized into Christianity and the church. As I began to understand that, I began to see that our way of praying is a Creator-centred spirituality.

I never cease to be amazed at the wonder of our God and Creator. When I pray in the four directions, I think of Revelation 7:1, of the angels in the four directions. Verse 9 tells me that it is okay to pray to the great circle of Elders. When I pray in the four directions, I pray for the protection of mother earth who gives us the clothes we wear. All the synthetics that we wear, all the metals that we use come from the earth. Human beings don't create anything; we only change the forms.

Those of us who are recovering our Native spirituality must proceed cautiously. We must be sensitive to our brothers and sisters. Some have been taught our Native ways are wrong. Some people feel that these ways can't come together. It is true that we must be cautious and discerning as we bring back our culture and traditions, but I know our God and Creator can do many things.

The vision that I have when I look ahead is a beautiful vision of a Native church where we will look after each other. It is so good to be here and to see some of you priests and speakers need interpreters. Their own languages are honoured. I pray that we will have open minds and do good things, that we will bless and purify each other and help each other.

When we untie the apron strings, we must cut them off at the apron and use them to bind us together in love so that we may be open, caring, and sharing—working for the Creator.

8 / AN APOLOGY FROM THE PRIMATE

Following the reflections by ecumenical and international partners reported in chapter 7, the evening began with a healing service. Prior to the service, Archbishop Michael Peers requested permission to speak to the gathering.

A MESSAGE FROM THE PRIMATE
OF THE ANGLICAN CHURCH OF CANADA
Minaki, Ontario. Friday, August 6, 1993

My Brothers and Sisters:
Together here with you I have listened as you have told your stories of the residential schools.

I have heard the voices that have spoken of pain and hurt experienced in the schools, and of the scars which endure to this day.

I have felt shame and humiliation as I have heard of suffering inflicted by my people and as I think of the part our church played in that suffering.

I am deeply conscious of the sacredness of the stories that you have told, and I hold in the highest honour those who have told them.

I have heard with admiration the stories of people and communities who have worked at healing, and I am aware of how much more healing is needed.

I also know that I am in need of healing, and my own people are in need of healing, and our church is in need of healing. Without that healing we will continue the same attitudes that have done such damage in the past.

I know that healing takes a long time, both for people and for communities.

I also know that it is God who heals and that God can begin to heal when we open ourselves, our wounds, our failure, and our shame, to God. I want to take one step along that path here and now.

I accept and I confess, before God and you, our failures in the residential schools. We failed you. We failed ourselves. We failed God.

I am sorry, more than I can say, that we were a part of a system which took you and your children from home and family.

I am sorry, more than I can say, that we tried to remake you in our image, taking from you your language and the signs of your identity.

I am sorry, more than I can say, that in our schools so many were abused physically, sexually, culturally, and emotionally.

On behalf of the Anglican Church of Canada, I present our apology.

I do this at the desire of those in the Church, like the National Executive Council, who know some of your stories and have asked me to apologize.

I do this in the name of many who do not know these stories.

And I do this even though there are those in the church who cannot accept the fact that these things were done in our name.

As soon as I am home, I shall tell all the bishops what I have said, and ask them to co-operate with me and with the National Executive Council in helping this healing at the local level. Some bishops have already begun this work.

I know how often you have heard words which have been empty because they have not been accompanied by actions. I pledge to you my best efforts, and the efforts of our church at the national level, to walk with you along the path of God's healing.

The work of the Residential Schools Working Group, the video, the commitment and the effort of the Special Assistants to the Primate for this work, and the grants available for healing conferences are some signs of that pledge; and we shall work for others.

This is Friday, the day of Jesus' suffering and death. It is the anniversary of the first atomic bomb at Hiroshima, one of the most terrible injuries ever inflicted by one people on another.

But even atomic bombs and Good Friday are not the last word. God raised Jesus from the dead as a sign that life and wholeness are the everlasting and unquenchable purpose of God.

Thank you for listening to me.

+ Michael
Archbishop and Primate

Following the apology, Dominic Eshkakagon asked Michael Peers to come forward to receive prayers for healing in a traditional ceremony that opened with sweetgrass. The primate then led one of four prayer teams, each of which was composed of three people: a clergyperson, an Elder, and a youth participant. The prayer teams each faced the Traditional Four Directions and offered healing and anointing to participants. Candles were lit in the four directions at the centre of the room. Many people came forward for prayers for healing.

Keepers of the Memory met long into the following night. Their responses are reflective of the deep emotion of the gathering:

When I heard the apology, I couldn't stop crying.

I enjoyed everything that happened today. The speakers presented their own stories from their own communities and countries. I was touched by what the primate had to say to us. I was touched by the healing service. I was most touched to see other young people cry. I felt the Spirit moving.

In our small groups, we are looking at directions of the future. It's up to us to work on those directions, to bring healing to our communities.

Ecumenical and international partners gave us a glimpse of a vision of what our church can be, our Native church. The apology today set everything in motion. We can now start working on our vision, clarifying it and bringing it into being.

The healing service was very appropriate. It used the Four Directions of our Traditions. It was very appropriate, very meaningful.

The healing process takes a long time. We still have a lot of pain ahead. We have to start believing we are the church in our own right and on our own merit.

Every day, different things are revealed. The blending of Native Traditions and Christianity has been my dream. I'd like to see it happen more and more in the future. Every time I see blending of traditions, I have good feelings.

I'm looking for my roots—and every day my roots are opening to me.

I'm going to take a lot back to my church and community.

The events of the week had an enormous impact on the thirteen non-Aboriginal people invited by the National Executive Council to attend. They participated in small groups and met daily to discuss their own responses to events of the week in order both to prepare for their collective report to National Executive Council and to share what they felt needed to happen individually. One such response was that of Bryan Bjerring, a representative of the Diocese of Rupert's Land.

A REFLECTION AND A PLEDGE
by Bryan Bjerring

I suppose that in the archives of the Anglican Church of Canada, this event will be recorded as the Second National Native Convocation of the Anglican Church of Canada. For me, it will be the Residential Schools Convocation. It was here, this week, that what I had known in my head became as well a matter of the heart and of the soul.

To hear about the pain associated with residential schools run by and in the name of my church—our church—and in some sense to know in graphically personal ways that pain, has deeply affected me.

In this sense, words really do fail me. What can I say about that experience that First Nations people have not already said? The refrain throughout the week has been, for me, the incarceration and brutalization of children.

We say that scripture records the relationship between God and God's people. That story continues to be told in history, in the story of humankind, both individually and corporately. The New Zealand Liturgy concludes readings from scripture with the words, "Hear what the Spirit is saying to the Church." These words apply equally to what the Spirit has said to the church through and by the residential schools experience and the work of this week.

For me the answer is justice which will be the work of a lifetime. I am grateful that, because of the invitation extended to me to be present here, I have been given a small role in this.

I commit myself to working at ways which will allow the story to be told to the people of Rupert's Land and to sharing my experience of this week with non-Aboriginal Christians.

I also commit myself, upon the invitation of the First Nations people of the Diocese of Rupert's Land, to working with them in a ministry of healing and reconciliation.

Thank you for listening to me, especially when hundreds of people, my kind of people, were not prepared to listen to you.

Non-Native participants shared their concerns, their under-standings, their responses. It was clear that the systemic abuses had to be acknowledged. It was understood that residential schools were a product of the time. Anne Davidson, a non-Aboriginal member of National Executive Council grew up in Britain. She noted that for many generations in England, boarding schools were considered the best way of educating children. Many peo-ple who did not have bad intentions were working within the schools and churches. Nevertheless, it was clear that healing needed to happen.

Being a non-Native person of the race that perpetuated [the residential school system], I think of the words of Jesus on the cross: "Father, for-give them, for they know not what they do." All things considered, all the abuse, the people that perpetuated it—some were evil, but some weren't. It was a system of a colonial government which perpetuated itself and a product of a culture which sent its own children away.

It was a product of the time. Now, we see it was bad, it was wrong. I feel shame for it. But the pain and the anguish these children have carried with them through their lives has got to be healed.

The non-Native convocation participants took five resolutions to the church's National Executive Council. The resolutions asked the National Executive Council to

• *allocate from funds designated for Anglican Appeal a substan-tial amount for healing ministries related to survivors of residen-tial schools and their families.*

• *continue the process of providing support for the Council of Na-tive Ministries Residential Schools Task Force and Living Waters.*

• *direct the National Program Committee to take charge of the work of educating non-Native peoples on residential schools is-sues.*

• *request appropriate persons, committees, and agencies to act as advocates regarding the post-secondary education issue.*

• *establish a memorial fund for bursaries for Native people who seek further (non-degree) education or training to enable healing work within their communities.*

In addition to the formal recommendations, non-Native delegates individually made many commitments to assist understanding in their own communities and dioceses. Their intent was to share the experience in their parishes, with family and friends, and with editors of diocesan papers, and to support efforts of their local native councils to bring healing to their communities.

9 / A CELEBRATION OF THE HUMAN SPIRIT

The ceremony of purification, perhaps the most ancient ceremony of our Anishinabe people, is a simple ceremony done at every gathering of our people.

In this purification ceremony we come together to prepare ourselves to be together. Our people have always prayed for open minds. We pray for open eyes that we may see good in all that happens. We pray that our mouths will speak well of others and that our hearts will be pure so that we will love and care for others. We ask for purification of our minds and bodies so that we will serve well.

Our Lord Jesus taught us to pray to our Father in heaven as he himself did. We remember also that he said that when two or three are gathered, he will be with us and grant our prayers. This purification ceremony is above all a prayer from the heart, a prayer that we will be able to serve our brothers and sisters and all Creation with good clear minds. When we call upon God, we always know that what we do is going to be right and good.

Dominic Eshkakagon

Today we can start dancing the dream.

A Keeper of the Memory
Second National Native Convocation

n the last days of the convocation, there were many moments of sharing, reconciliation, laughter, and celebration. The question *What do we need for our healing?* called for a deep examination within all persons: an examination of what they longed for in their own communities to assist in the healing process, as well as an examination of the possible responses of the church.

Participants had been formed into small groups throughout the week. Those groups reported back to the larger group; their suggestions were thoughtful, creative, and hope filled. They wished that the sharing which had begun at the convocation be continued in their communities. They believed that communication includes both talking and listening. Groups stressed the importance of directing support from the church to the people who need it most.

There was a longing for resolution of the struggle between Native Tradition spirituality and Christianity. It was suggested that Native spiritual Traditions should be used in Christian healing. It was felt that communities should draw on the Traditional help from the Elders which was a part of their culture. Positive two-way communication between youth and Elders was encouraged.

Groups affirmed the apology as an important step to begin the healing process. Many called for action in the form of financial support to assist with recovery of the spirituality and culture which had been lost through the policies of government and the discouragement of language and culture in many residential schools. It was helpful to many to understand what the assimilation policy was designed to do and the suffering it caused and to learn from the past. It was suggested that a day of the year be set aside to remember brothers and sisters who died in the residential schools.

All agreed that we need to learn to laugh, to find ways to encourage humour, sharing, and lightness. We need to love each other and help each other. More teachings of Traditional ways were affirmed as a way of involving and assisting young people in taking pride in their heritage. There was encouragement for involving young people in decision making.

Sensitizing leaders to the problems, concerns, and gifts of the community was affirmed. There was recognition of the need to raise and question the presence of racism. The establishment of healing centres was encouraged. Above all, it was felt that as a communion we are to walk side by side as we seek to discern God's will in the changing relationship between Native peoples and the church.

While much remains to be done, the participants felt that a great deal of healing had begun at the convocation. Tired but hopeful, they gathered for the final ceremony at the lakeshore on a hillside looking out over the waters. Priests, Elders, and lay leaders processed down the hill to the altar swathed in a star blanket. The sun shone and glistened on the waters as the readers, draped in the colours of the four directions, said prayers facing in each of them. Mervin Wolfleg sang a song for healing from atop a hill behind the gathering. The homily, by Michael Peers, encouraged all to continue the work of healing and reconciliation in their home communities.

WE ARE THE WOUNDED HEALERS
A reflection by the Most Reverend Michael Peers

I came to the convocation five years ago as the only non-Aboriginal person. I was invited to speak at the beginning, to speak at the end, and not to speak in between. This gave me a lot of time to think; and when it came to the reflection at the closing service, I spoke for too long.

This time, there was a difference. You have invited a number of people to be part of the convocation and to be partners with you from other churches. My reflection is about one personal incident, and it has to do with the passage of the gospel where Jesus sent his people out.

Last night an unexpected thing happened. Last night what I had expected was the opportunity to deliver an apology from the church and from myself, and it was also my intention to present myself to those of you who were administering healing rites. I didn't realize I would immediately be asked to join part of a group taking part in the healing. This is also significant because I was asked to be in the West.

The spirituality invoked in the West is introspection, the balancing of emotions in a spirit of gentleness, and I am an introspective person. To me it is quite an amazing thing that happened at the close of the event – going from [being] a person who has publicly asked for healing, to [being] a person who presents himself for healing, to being asked then to be a healer.

But it is the way that God deals with us. It makes me think of a book called *The Wounded Healer* that takes its theme from the person of Christ, both wounded and healer. Many other Christians have spoken of it. We have often moaned that we are both wounded and that we are healers, that we might become contributors to the healing process. The truth is that we are both at the same time. The world is not divided between the wounded and the healers, but each of us is both at the same time. We know that because we are followers of Jesus.

The first thing Jesus did with his disciples after his resurrection was to show them his wounded hands and side and say, "Peace be with you." The wounds and the peace went together. God had raised him from the dead but had not removed the wounds. They remained and were the sign that it was Jesus. He then said to his disciples, "As the father has sent me, so I sent you." He sent Jesus as healer, but as wounded healer. When he said, "*As* the Father sent me, so I send you," he meant, "in the same way that the Father sent me, with the same power as the Father gave me."

Those words were spoken to us—to all of us and to each of us. We are sent from here with the same power as Jesus gave to his disciples, as the Father had given him; and we have the same calling. The calling is to be healers, even though we are wounded, and more than that, to be healers *because*. This reflection helps me when I am feeling more wounded than healer.

It is very easy for it to all to become an enormous burden. And so I encourage you to understand that you are not just one person when you leave; you are part of a community, and you are a part of every follower of Christ that has ever been. Remember that when we go away and we are on our own, everyone is still with you. Every person here is a resource, and every resource God gave to Jesus in his earthly ministry is available to each of you as the church. Every resource, every power is available. When you feel yourself to be isolated and wounded by that isolation, remember that you have been incorporated in this amazing community called the church.

Receive the Holy Spirit and the power to make that real. Here each of us is wounded and all of us are in need of healing. We are called in power to be healers. The good news is that we are together today and that while we may be separated tomorrow we are still together day after day.

May God give you strength and make you a blessing so that you know yourselves to be both wounded and healers. It is a privilege

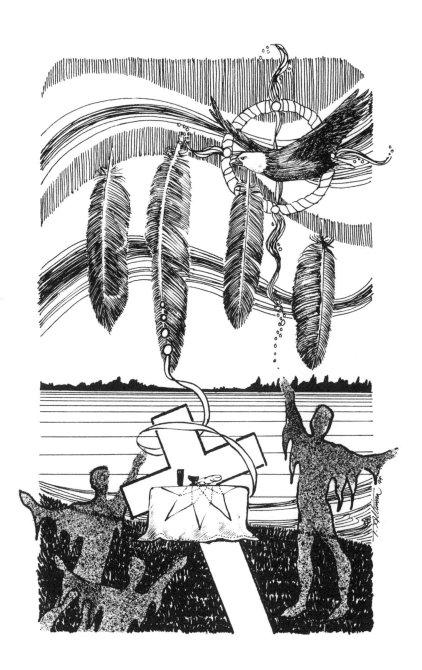

for me to know myself as at one and the same time both wounded and healer.

The Elders had met and discussed long into the night their response to the apology. Although some expressed fear about not knowing what those who were not at the event might think of the apology, the overwhelming desire of the Elders Council was to accept the apology. A bald eagle, the symbol of healing, which had flown gracefully over the lake behind the primate as he spoke, continued to circle as Vi Smith came forward to speak to the primate on behalf of the Elders.

On behalf of this gathering, we acknowledge and accept the apology that the primate has offered on behalf of the Anglican Church of Canada.

It was offered from his heart with sincerity, sensitivity, compassion, and humility. We receive it in the same manner. We offer praise and thanks to our Creator for his courage. We know it wasn't easy. Let us keep him in our hearts and prayers, that God will continue to give him the strength and courage to continue with his tasks.

The eucharist was celebrated by the Reverend Laverne Jacobs. Traditional ceremonies were incorporated through the eucharistic prayer. At the conclusion of the final hymn, many paused, looking over glistening waters as the eagle continued to soar.

The day which had begun with worship on the theme *Thank you as we search for healing* ended in celebration, with singing, dancing, and laughter, led by master of ceremonies, James Jeffries. Episcopal partner from the United States, Ginny Doctor presented James Isbister with a "noisemaker" to encourage the work of the Council for Native Ministries. There was much rejoicing and many happy moments of shared experiences as the community time drew to a close.

The day was truly one of thanksgiving. Earlier, youth delegates gave thanks for laughter, tears, frustrations, shared dreams, and listening. They were appreciative of the freedom to question, the start of healing, and friendship. They offered challenges and a prayer and presented a gift to Dominic Eshkakagon. As he was receiving this gift, Dominic expressed a conviction shared by all: "It is a sign of hope to see young people with us. Each time I listen to them talk, and have fun, it keeps me young at heart."

The final ceremony of the second convocation, *Dancing the Dream*, was a tree-planting ceremony. Convocation planners believed that at Minaki a strengthening of the dream would occur, and they understood this would be a sacred time. To mark the strengthening, they wished to place a living symbol at Minaki. A tree has special significance. The root is the foundation of the tree; roots have to be strong in order for a plant to survive and to be healthy. The tree symbolizes strength, connectedness to roots, and the need to be well grounded. For many Aboriginal people, being cut off from roots has been very painful; and so the tree with strong roots stands as an especially important symbol.

A large evergreen was purchased and named "dreamer" by the gathering. Delegates had been asked in advance to bring water to nourish the roots. After the blessing of the tree by Dominic, all took turns placing water brought from their home communities on the roots; they then took turns shovelling soil on the roots. The tree remains a physical reflection of the sacredness of the second convocation, the strengthening of the dream. The tree, connected to roots, reminded everyone of the importance of their spiritual roots. For many, re-acquainting themselves with roots is a symbol of life.

The tree as it grows is a visual sign, a symbol of life which marks and commemorates an event. Leaders believed that the strengthening of the dream at the second convocation led to the birthing of the new vision of partnership with the Anglican Church of Canada at the consultation in Winnipeg in April 1994.

10 / PARTNERSHIP

E ach person who attended the convocation will have his or her own reflections and story of growth which led to the vision of partnership. For Mervin Wolfleg the journey involved an integration of his respect for the primate, love of his children, and cultural understandings. Mervin had found the moment of the apology to be deeply disturbing. Months later at the Partners in Mission Consultation in Winnipeg where the new *Covenant* was signed, Mervin shared that this moment had troubled him greatly for a very long time; he had prayed about it, and pondered what it meant.

A REFLECTION ON THE PRIMATE'S APOLOGY
by Mervin Wolfleg

It was my children who helped me to deal with this, to understand this. In my tradition, it is important to learn from one's children. My children said, "The primate is a very good man. He is a very kind man and a strong man. So he could make the apology and it was the right thing to do." My children really believe this.

I wondered why my children would feel so differently about this apology. This question really bothered me. As I thought about it, I realized that my children—and children of today's generation— know what an apology means in the verbal tradition. In my own tradition, there are no words for "I'm sorry." Instead, an apology was more acted out than said. It was often a simple act of kindness, sometimes a gift or sometimes spending time with the other person to acknowledge that there has been a disagreement but that the disagreement shouldn't prevent continuing the important relationship. For example, when my father and I would have a disagreement, we would give each other time and space. In this time and space, we would work on the trust in the relationship. In the time and space, we would come to terms with what really happened. Then either one of us or both of us would move towards reconciliation in the form of either a gift or some time together. Such a small act of kindness served to cover the wound which was made.

This kind of teaching was taught to me as a young child and forms a part of our Traditional teachings and understandings. I tried to raise my children as Traditionally as I could, but what was missing were the nuances of the teaching, the understanding I had through the language and the daily act of living in the culture. I've taught my children the philosophy and the language of my people, but I had to do it in the English language.

My wife is from British Columbia and she also attended residential school. She was taken from her family younger than I and attended a residential school that was isolated and was very difficult. She didn't know her own language or culture. When we were married, I taught the culture to her as well as to my children.

I have taught my children the philosophy, the dances, the songs, and the culture. One of my boys has been a member of a Traditional society since he was four. What the children lack is language. There is a different way of trying to convey thoughts and feelings through language.

My first language is Siksika. The first language of my children is English; for some of them, their second language is French. My daughter studied French in school for seven years before going to university. She is now studying Siksika. The Siksika language is therefore her third language. My first language is her third language. Some of the younger children are studying Siksika in school and so understanding will be easier; but it remains their second language, while it is my first. This creates many differing understandings.

When my children discussed the apology with me, I felt they let me through a door of understanding. Most of the older people in our churches need to be aware that our children are not First Nations language speakers. This creates a somewhat different world view. Since it is also true that inculturation in a Tradition comes from the community in which one lives, sometimes children will do things in a Traditional way but will not realize that they are being Traditional. If they attend a school on the reserve, there are no problems. When they attend schools outside the reserve, they find that what is acceptable in an outside school is different than what is acceptable on the reserve. There is a cultural clash and it can be upsetting for them. It is sometimes hard to grasp that when their thought and language is in English, their values may still be Traditional. It is important to understand these differing understandings and world views so that they will be prepared to deal with the differences in cultures. As a counsellor, I have tried to help them with this.

There are differences between generations at times because our first languages are different. When our children speak English, we may assume they will have fewer problems as they move out into other communities, but they may still encounter cultural clashes there because the underlying values of our community are very deep.

Language is very important. When a language is not written down, it becomes a part of you. It is more alive; it is more real and more meaningful. The consequence of this is that people take more time for reflection. There is room for silence, for thought and reflection, in the Traditional world view. Then there is more taking on of responsibility for one's own life and actions. I believe this is true in cultures which have had oral traditions and it is similar to the Old Testament.

My feeling with the primate is that the pain needs to be acknowledged. To do so doesn't take away from the relationship—just as the pain our Saviour suffered for us has sustained our Christianity all these years. That pain has sustained a lot of growth.

Traditional people in my culture recognize that pain exists and is a part of life. This recognition is in part, I think, because in our culture life was sometimes very harsh before the coming of the missionaries and other Europeans. I think that is why the experience of residential school was accepted for a long time. Our people have now been in white society for many years, and this pain of residential schools has now been brought to the fore and is being discussed. I believe this is a part of the growth.

I needed an apology the instant after the first strap on my behind. I did not cry. I would not give them that satisfaction. If the white man inflicting the pain was truly Christian, he would have seen the one tear in my eye, and the fear. He would have felt some compassion and sorrow. He could have apologized then. Maybe that would have stopped the nine other straps. Maybe all the countless other straps my friends and I felt would never have fallen. I feel one human being cannot apologize for all the acts of violence committed by "Christian" white people against helpless Indian children. They failed their trust. Only Jesus can right the wrong. Has He? Who needs to ask for His forgiveness?

My feelings need truthful and direct expression which will only be when I share in my language with one of my Siksika brothers or sisters. I need to surrender the pain totally. I am impatient when I share and I have to be constantly interrupted to clarify my disclosures in English. At this point I have no choice. Others also need to disclose, and I long to hear their words. At times I even question if my experiences were real, but my feelings are still too real and frightening. My circle needs healing. I need affirmation.

When the primate apologized, I found myself somehow between my understanding of my own Traditional values and ways, which moved in me a strong feeling that it was wrong for the primate, a holy man, to be compromised and humiliated, and my own children, who are the future and who believed the primate was right to apologize. It was a simple, yet powerful, fulfilment of a vow of unconditional love—God's grace.

I feel right about the apology now, and I feel it is only right to walk in partnership from now on, taking full responsibility for our own spiritual lives.

Vi Samaha of the Nlha'7 kapmx First Nation and on the Council for Native Ministries has participated in both convocations. She echoes Mervin's belief in the importance of walking in partnership; she believes this partnership and taking fuller responsibility will bring healing. "Healing of communities," she says, "has to do with a strong sense of hope rooted in vision."

Vi grew up in an intergenerational family with strong ties between children and Elders and with an extended family firmly in place. Her observation is that as the community was gradually undermined, the response in the past was silence. Vi reflects on the silence of the past and her choice to break silence.

BREAKING THE SILENCE
by Vi Samaha

For generations my family and many others have chosen silence. While this was the choice of many generations, with the new partnership we are choosing not to be silent.

For many years I lived away from my community. Our families are very important to us; this has always been so. Youth are important;

Elders are important. The relationship between the two is critical for the health of our communities. One of the greatest tragedies over the past generations is that the relationships have been broken, especially those between the youth and the Elders. For generations there were no children in our communities. They were taken away to go to school. There was no laughter of children, no sounds of their playing.

Something new is being born. We're risking. We're breaking silence. We have to. The health of all of our children is at stake. Now we are hearing more and more the sounds of laughter of children in our midst. The whole purpose of this new partnership between Aboriginal peoples and the Anglican church is bound up also in bringing healing to our communities. We are spiritual people. We long for wholeness, for healing of broken hearts and broken relationships. As we hold up this vision of the future of communities, we have to hold before us the healing of our children.

When people came together for the Partners in Mission Consultation in Winnipeg, they hadn't planned the *Covenant.* It was something which evolved "as we were led by the Holy Spirit in the consultation," Donna Bomberry stated. "It was the right moment." Prior to the covenant signing, the leaders proclaimed their journey in this way:

OUR JOURNEY OF SPIRITUAL RENEWAL

We, the Indigenous partners in Canada of the Anglican Communion respectfully affirm our place in God's Creation and in God's Love, manifest through the Grace of Jesus Christ. In specific, we address the Anglican Canadians with whom we are in direct Communion.

We have shared a journey of close to three centuries in which we have been

- denied our place in God's Creation;
- denied our right as Children of God;
- treated as less than equal; and
- subjected to abuse, culturally, physically, emotionally, sexually, and spiritually.

The result, in our communities, homes, and daily lives, has been and continues to be

- broken homes and lives;
- sexual and family violence;
- high recidivism and incarceration;
- high chemical abuse;
- loss of spiritual fulfilment;
- loss of cultures, languages and traditions; and
- poor stewardship of Mother Earth.

Because the National Church's canons, structure, and policies have not always responded to our needs nor heard our voice, we now claim our place and responsibility as equal partners in a new shared journey of healing moving towards wholeness and justice.

We acknowledge that God is calling us to a prayerful dialogue towards self-determination for us, the Indigenous People, within the Anglican Communion in Canada. Through this new relationship we can better respond to the challenges facing us in a relevant and meaningful way.

As faithful people of God, guided by the Holy Spirit, we invite you, the Anglican Communion of Canada, to covenant with us, the Indigenous Anglicans of Canada, in our vision of a new and enriched journey.

When the members of the Council for Native Ministries came away from the covenant signing in Winnipeg and understood the significance of the event, they wanted to mark the place and give recognition to the sacredness of the event and the place. A tree planting ceremony took place at St. Benedict's on the outskirts of Winnipeg, Manitoba, following a sunrise ceremony led by Mervin Wolfleg at the Council for Native Ministries meeting on October 30, 1994. Watering of the tree was in the Four Directions of Native Tradition.

Speaking of the ceremony, Donna Bomberry, chairperson of the Council for Native Ministries stated, "We felt it was important to leave something of ourselves there for others to enjoy as it grows. We wished them to know we appreciated their hospitality and the environment and atmosphere that was sacred which surrounded our meeting—and we honour that."

The trees hold many meanings for those who were present. Perhaps most important is the strong awareness of the need for affirmation of rootedness in their own spiritual traditions, connectedness to creation and to each other, and the new strength they bring to the Anglican communion in sharing their spirituality. Donna Bomberry has stated, "It is helpful for all to understand this new 'birthing' and vision of health within communities is rooted in traditions which have always been present."

The Council for Native Ministries celebrates the new partnership with the church. The affirmation of identity, the determination to maintain a unique spirituality, and the recognition of the distinctive and unique gifts of Aboriginal people point to a different future. The relationship is now one of trust, acceptance, and openness. Partnership enables First Nations people to be the people the Creator intended us to be within the life of the church. In the words of Maori Bishop Hui Vercoe of Aotearoa (New Zealand), who participated in the second convocation, "The thing that binds us together is that we believe in one God, but we do it in our own way, in our own time, and with our own traditions."

APPENDIX I
THE DEVELOPMENT OF CHURCH-RUN RESIDENTIAL SCHOOLS

This material has been adapted from the *Royal Commission on Aboriginal People: a Special Consultation with Historic Mission Churches,* prepared by Terry Thompson with John Bird in 1993.

An Overview of the Early Mission Period

The relationship between First Nations and the Anglican Church began in 1753 in Atlantic Canada with the appointment of the Reverend Thomas Wood as a missionary to the Micmac people. He was sponsored by the Society for the Propagation of the Gospel (SPG), an independent church missionary society in Britain. The Bishop of Litchfield and Coventry, writing in an SPG pamphlet of 1756, expressed a common view:

How can it be supposed that the untutored mind of a poor Indian should be capable of imbibing the truths, or digesting the precepts of the Gospel, however plainly proposed to him?

But first civilize the barbarians by friendly intercourse and gentle treatment; let them see and partake of the good effects of Christianity in our honesty and justice; calm their savage dispositions, and rescue them out of that wildness they have unhappily fallen into; and then we shall find them well prepared for the reception of the truth.

Much that followed, including the establishment of residential schools, was based on this view of First Nations people.

A variety of initiatives followed. In 1786 the New England Company began to employ Anglican mission agents in New Brunswick. In Upper Canada the first Aboriginal Anglicans were loyalists who arrived as refugees from the American War of Independence. Anglican Mohawks established settlements on the Bay of Quinte and at Brantford, where they built the first Protestant church. Aboriginal lay readers provided regular Sunday services which were supplemented by semi-annual visits from Anglican clergy. In 1827 the New England Company began to work in the Rice Lake area and in 1829 took over responsibility for providing clergy along the Grand River.

This first generation of missionary effort produced Native Christians who became missionaries to their own people. Aboriginal church leaders such as Augustin Shingwauk of the Great Lakes Anishinabe and Thomas Vincent of the James Bay Cree also acted as political advocates in their people's relations with the developing colonial administrations.

In the area of Red River (now Winnipeg) and on the Prairies, there was a significant time lag between Aboriginal contact with traders and the arrival of Anglican missionaries. When the first missionaries arrived in 1820, the Hudson Bay Company had been operating in the area for about 150 years. Missionaries and Aboriginals together established the system of syllabic writing still in use among Cree Christians.

In British Columbia the first Anglican chaplain was Herbert Beaver, who arrived in 1836. Missionaries and the First Nations peoples of the West Coast clashed seriously over Traditional religious practices, notably the potlatch. Even during this time, however, Anglican missionaries generally recognized and supported the Aboriginal peoples' rights to their traditional lands.

A Shift in Focus: Residential Schools

A major change in missionary policy in the mid-nineteenth century was the move to establish residential schools. This was partly the result of a perception among mission workers that it was more productive to focus on converting Aboriginal children than to try to convert the adults. This change had a profound impact on Aboriginal people, as it reduced their input into the missionary project and discouraged the further development of Indigenous Anglican leadership.

In 1820 John West became the first Church Missionary Society missionary in Canada. On his way to his posting as the Hudson Bay Chaplain at Red River, he took several Aboriginal children, from as far away as York Factory on Hudson Bay, and established the first Anglican residential school for Native people. In his diary he wrote:

I spoke to an Indian, called Withaweecapo, about taking two of his boys to the Red River Colony with me to educate and maintain. . . . I had to establish the principle that the North American Indian of these regions would part from his children, to be educated in the white man's knowledge and religion.

In the next 150 years the Anglican Church in Canada opened and administered more than twenty-six Indian Residential Schools, as they were commonly known. These schools were generally funded by the federal government, which shared the goal to "Christianize" and "civilize" First Nations people. The children were taken from their families and communities and put in a residential setting where, in the case of the Anglican Church, they were provided with a British and Anglican education.

The intention and the effect of residential schooling was to cut Native children off from their own cultures, languages, and lifestyles. The expected outcome was the disappearance of Aboriginal culture, language, religion, and values and the absorption of First Nations people into the mainstream Anglo-Canadian culture, generally at the bottom end of the labouring classes as farm workers or domestic servants.

Sidney Gould, the second General Secretary of the Missionary Society of the Church of England in Canada, the church structure that administered the Anglican residential schools, in 1924 stated the aims of both church and society:

Canada is and must increasingly become . . . a country of white men rooted and grounded in those fundamental scriptural conceptions of the individual, of society, (and) of the state . . . as the same have been conceived and found expression through the struggles and conquests of the several peoples of British blood and traditions.

Some Aboriginal leaders, recognizing the need for their children to become familiar with the settlers' language and culture and wanting them to have a Christian education, had encouraged the establishment of residential schools. More commonly, the schools were imposed on the people out of a sense of mission and with little or no consultation. The church and the Canadian government worked as partners and decision makers in the administration and funding of the schools, with the overall aim of assimilation or "cultural replacement."

Residential schools had problems from the beginning because parents were disinclined to trust their children to an alien culture. Some schools had high numbers of children with physical and emotional problems. In a school near Calgary, up to 25 percent of the students died.

In 1910 the Church Missionary Society in England decided to turn the administration of its Canadian missions over to the local dioceses. Most of the missions were located on reserves and, in addition to churches, included small day schools as well as the more prevalent residential schools. To ease the burden on local dioceses, the Mission Society of the Canadian church established the Indian Residential Schools Commission, which took over administration of the schools in 1919.

The federal government sought to maintain a Christian influence in the schools. The "industrial" nature of the curriculum, and its assimilationist objectives, were clear. The bishops were

to provide at the said school teachers and officers qualified to give the pupils religious instruction at proper times; to instruct the male pupils of the said school in gardening, farming and in the care of livestock, or other such industries as are suitable to their local requirements; to instruct the female pupils in cooking, laundry work, needlework, general housewifery and dairy work, where such dairy work can be carried on; to teach all the pupils the ordinary branches of an English education; calisthenics, physical drill and fire drill; to teach the effects of alcoholic drinks and narcotics on the human system, and how to live in a healthy manner; to instruct the older advanced pupils in the duties and privileges of British citizenship, explaining to them the fundamental principles of the Government of Canada, and to train them in such knowledge and appreciation of Canada as will inspire them with respect and affection for our country and its laws.

(Memorandum of agreement between the Department of Indian Affairs and various dioceses, 1910)

The relationship between the federal government and the churches contracted to run the residential schools continued until 1970 when the last of the residential schools was closed. Over 150 years, a total of eighty-five residential schools were run by the different denominations. Thousands of children were removed from their homes and placed in the schools. Some lost language and culture. Some returned to their homes after many years unable to communicate even with their own parents.

A Change in Direction

The phasing out of residential schools and the rapid political changes of the 1960s challenged the Anglican Church to re-examine the theology and approach to mission that had governed its relationship with Aboriginal peoples. The civil rights movement in the United States, led by Martin Luther King Jr., had a profound effect on many people. Anglican leaders began to recognize that First Nations had been severely marginalized and oppressed throughout Canadian history. They also began to see the church's complicity.

Charles Hendry made a detailed examination of the relationship between the Anglican Church of Canada and the Aboriginal peoples. In *Beyond Traplines*, tabled at General Synod in 1969, Hendry reported:

Many informants interviewed, who were former residential school pupils, have revealed a common thread of resentment and bitterness running through the accounts given of their school days.

They spoke of boys and girls being whipped or slapped when they spoke their Native language. The aim was to make the children speak English. They told of being taught to despise the way of life of their parents as pagan and disagreeable; and spoke of being absent from home for ten months of the year, or for several years.

The changes brought about by the Hendry report began a new relationship between church and Native peoples—a relationship which has been evolving over decades (see chapter 3). It was not until the Second National Native Convocation, however, that the pain of residential school experiences began to be disclosed and shared openly by many of the people who had endured them. This powerful and historic gathering launched a new journey toward healing and partnership for Native peoples and the Anglican Church of Canada.

APPENDIX II
PRAYERS AND RESOURCES

Prayers and Reflections
Throughout the second convocation, prayers and reflections, offered sometimes in English and sometimes in languages of First Nations peoples, nurtured and sustained the gathering. Some examples are provided below.

A Reflection from the Youth
by Dwayne Lyons

We, the youth, have learned many things this week.

We have learned that we have a voice amongst the older people and within the church.

We have also learned about love and fear, pain and joy, patience, respect and friendship, that age makes no difference as we all have common bonds and ties to each other.

Finally, we have learned that God is always among us (Amen to that, Brother).
Thank you.

Inuktitut Blessing
by Daniel Aupalu

Quviasukpunga Ullumi
Nunalituqatsajaungitut
Tuqisivaliamata Nunalituqatsajait
Anniagutinqinik, Quviasukpungalu
Inuitlu Allailu
Katutjiqatigipaliangmata
Pinasuarnimigut

translation:
I'm glad today that non-Aboriginal people are understanding more about the pains of the Aboriginal people; and also, I'm happy that the Aboriginals, including Inuit, are working together more and more.

Cree Blessing
translated by James Isbister

Kisemanito Ki wicewikonaw
ki kiskinohtahikonaw
ki sawenimikonaw
Tahto kiskaw ota aski
e-pimohteyak

God be with us.
He will lead us,
He will bless us
Every day on this earth
As we walk on this earth.

God Save the World
by Edna Masuko, Africa

(From Luke 4:16-22)

If you believe and I believe
And we together pray,
The Holy Spirit will come down
And God will set people free.
The Holy Spirit will come down
And God will set people free.

For the past two years an ecumenical publication, *The Dancing Sun,* has been co-published by First Nations Ecumenical Liturgical Resources, History and Publications Board, and the Division of Mission in Canada of the United Church of Canada. Anglican funding and support have been supplied by the Council for Native Ministries, the Partners in Canadian Mission Unit, and the Diocese of Rupert's Land. *Dancing Sun* materials are developed within Aboriginal communities and reflect their cultural traditions and experience. The resource is available through the Anglican Book Centre or through United Church Book Rooms. Editions of *The Dancing Sun* now available are

The Dancing Sun I: An Advent Resource
The Dancing Sun II: A Lent-Easter Resource
The Dancing Sun III: Vacation Bible School Resource
The Dancing Sun IV: Strengthening Families
The Dancing Sun V: Grief in the Aboriginal Community
The Dancing Sun VI: Journeys in Spirituality: Stories from
      Christian Indigenous People (available June 1995)

The following prayers have been selected from numbers II, IV, and V.

The Dancing Sun II: A Lent-Easter Resource

Creator,
we are made in your image.
May we allow your love to reach every part of our lives,
remembering that what we do is not only for ourselves,
for our families and our communities—
it is also that our lives may be lived
in more perfect service to you.

Creator,
you are with us always.
    You hear our cries—and forgive us.
We give thanks for the beauty of creation,
    for the gift of life itself.
May we, understanding the gift of your Son,
    find your new life as we walk our own journeys.

Creator,
we give thanks for all teachings which bring life and healing.
We give thanks for the good teachings of our ancestors—
and for the new life brought through teachings of Christ.
We long for healing in our communities.
May we respect each other as we search for your way.
May we be guided by your love.

Creator God,
we give thanks that whatever we do, wherever we go,
    you are with us always.
Your hand guides us and will lead us to a place of healing.
May we stand firm in the knowledge that your intention
    is that we be healed and whole—
    that we experience your resurrection.
May we rest in the truth of your love
    and care for all of your daughters and sons . . .
    (say aloud the name of each participant)

The Dancing Sun IV: Strengthening Families

Creator, we long for wholeness in our families,
    for honest, open communication
    to say what we need to say
    in safety and without fear.

Refrain: *Hear our Prayer, O God,*
    and in your love, answer.

Creator, help us to stay close
    to never let go of one another
    in joy as well as in pain
    to embrace
    to feel the physical presence of one another
    and be really present, one to another.

Refrain: *Hear our Prayer, O God,*
    and in your love, answer.

Creator, we need to feel connected
    to our families
    to the church family
    to learn and to grow
    to be part of a web of relationships
    to pass on values, love and a sense of closeness
    to be part of an inner circle of safety,
    spiraling out to an open circle to allow others in.

Refrain: *Hear our Prayer, O God,*
  and in your love, answer.

Creator, we long for a gentler time
  of warmth and wholeness
  for time and energy to nourish families
  for honest sharing
  out of genuine love for all family members.

Refrain: *Hear our Prayer, O God,*
  and in your love, answer.

Creator, we long to dance
  to move into the centre of the circle
  to touch and grow together in community
  into completeness.

Refrain: *Hear our Prayer, O God,*
  and in your love, answer.

The Dancing Sun V: Grief in the Aboriginal Community

Creator, we thank you
that there are different paths to wholeness.

We see your wonder in creation all around us,
in the singing birds and the flowing water.

We give thanks for the opportunity to share,
and for everything that the Creator has given us.

We give thanks for connectedness to each other,
and to all Creation, the whole created world.

We give thanks that Jesus Christ
has been in our past and is in our present
and will be with us in our future.

We give thanks for laughter, for humour,
for the many different ways that we are able to be together,
and to be in community.

We give thanks for the differences between us
and for the respect we have for different paths.

We give thanks for the Elders,
the opportunities to be respected no matter what our views
and to celebrate the different views that we have.

We give thanks for different approaches to grief,
and for the sharing, and the opportunities to laugh
and to share and to care
and that we are each different and yet together.

We give thanks for new understandings,
for the bridges we are able to build between people.

Help us to be open to new life and to vision,
to bring new life to our homes,
to our families and to our communities.

An Interactive Exercise
The following interactive community experience was first shared
by Ms. Ginny Doctor, an Episcopal Church Partner at the *Dancing
the Dream* convocation, and then facilitated by Ms. Donna
Bomberry, chair of the Council for Native Ministries, at the Partners in Mission consultation in Winnipeg, April 1994, where it
was greatly appreciated by Aboriginal leaders. It is reprinted
here with permission and at the request of people who found it
helpful at the latter event.

Adapt the exercise to suit the needs of your group. You may
wish to use seven different readers for the responses to Christ's
words, as the script suggests, or you may have the narrator read
the words of Christ with one other person reading the responses.

Jumping Off the Cradleboard: Releasing Our Future
The concept for this exercise is based on the unbinding ceremony at the Anglican Encounter in Salvadore, Brazil, in 1992.
The Reverend Victor Li of Toronto, Ontario, has written an English version based on his reflection on the unbinding ceremony
which was originally presented in Portuguese. The Reverend Mr.
Li prepared his version specifically for Good Friday and Easter
services. He has used it in presentations reporting on the confer-

ence in Brazil. For his original version, Mr. Li may be contacted through the Diocese of Toronto.

The exercise has been adapted by Ginny Doctor, an Episcopal Church (U.S.A.) missionary to the Diocese of Alaska. Donna Bomberry further adapted the exercise for use with the Aboriginal community at the Partners in Mission consultation in Winnipeg. The exercise was arranged for this publication by Donna Bomberry and Teresa Mandricks.

Cradleboard materials required
- a cardboard box, dismantled and large enough that, flat, it is at least the length of a standing man (babe)
- twine rope, enough to fasten the cardboard cradleboard, crudely, to the standing babe
- a blanket in which to wrap the babe
- a hooded shirt or jacket for the babe

LEADER:
For a minute I'd like you to imagine yourself on a cradleboard. In years gone by, think how it was for our ancestors when they were here. Imagine yourself on this cradleboard, with your legs strapped, your feet against the hard board, your arms strapped, wrapped in an old army blanket, and remember the moss stuck between your legs to hold your waste.

When you are there on that cradleboard, you can't move. You can't use your hands to scratch those mosquito bites on your forehead. All you can do is move your eyes, your mouth, and listen with your ears. Does it seem hard to you? It does to me.

But does it seem it would be safe and secure on that cradleboard where your mother put you? Do you think you'll be safe and secure there? Can you feel the warmth of your mother's body?

What do your eyes see as you look around? Remember that your eyes are about the only thing that can move. What do they see? What do your ears hear? Remember, you're only a baby. What can you hear? What do you understand? What do you do with your mouth? Do you cry? Do you smile?

Think about it, how it must have been. I don't know if any of you were raised on a cradleboard, but I do know our grandparents were raised on a cradleboard. It is now only a reminder of what was, and I have heard it said that children who were raised on the cradleboard were more perceptive and more observant. In those years, the babies were left there until they could walk.

Now, I want you to think about this cradleboard more abstractly. For many of us the term "cradleboard" has come to mean a dependence upon someone or something else. We wait for someone else to do it. We wait for someone else to say, "Yes, you can do it." We wait for someone to hold our hand, to show us the way.

Guess what? Many of us are still waiting. It is time for us to jump off the cradleboard and reclaim our responsibility for ourselves, each other, and our ministry. It may be safe and secure upon that cradleboard, but I am here to tell you that the more you move the longer you are going to live. And it is a life that we can control—instead of it controlling us. Think about all of this as we present to you the bundling of the babe.

Silence

LEADER:
A few of us here witnessed at the Worldwide Anglican Encounter in Brazil a similar binding of humanity. It is not meant to offend our ancestors or ourselves. Times have changed. Let this experience be a liberating experience. Think of it symbolically, visually studying our hearts and spirits.

There will come a time when you will be asked to participate. If you are moved to do it, please do it.

A person is led in by a dozen or so women who proceed (during the readings, as directed below) to strap him/her onto the cardboard "cradleboard," tying him with the twine.

LEADER:
Jesus' first word on the cross: "Father, forgive them for they know not what they do."

(Babe stands dressed before cradleboard)

FIRST READER:
"Why? What evil has been done?" Pilate asked that question, but the voice of the crowd drowned out his voice. Why? What evil have they done?

What evil have the little Indian children done that they should suffer?

The hands of Christ were pierced by nails; our hands, the hands of the ancients and of helpless victims, are also being pierced by violence, hatred, oppression, and racism. Our hands lie still, bound against the body, and cannot reach out in love and compassion and touch those who need comforting and counselling. Lord Jesus, it is hard to ask for God's forgiveness, especially when our persecutors show no signs of repentance. Is it just ignorance on their part? Lord Jesus, you stretched out your loving arms on the cross to save us. Stretch them again to embrace us.

Silence for reflection

LEADER:
Jesus' second word on the Cross: "Today you will be with me in Paradise."

(Blanket is draped and board is tied up to babe)

SECOND READER:
Why? What evil has been done? What evil has she done? Our feet are bound, our ability to move is limited. How can we be with you in paradise? We are stuck in Hell! We follow your footsteps with our eyes and find our way to the cross.

Indian people in today's world are being trampled by the oppressive weight of poverty and economic injustice. Our people in the poorer parts of Indian Country are not the only ones; there are less visible poor and vulnerable people in our midst, being marginalized, left out, kept out. Food banks do not belong to paradise. Our people are oppressed by economic hardship. Our people are less visible, in crisis intervention centres. Hotlines don't belong here in paradise. Life after death is fine for those who have a life before death; but not for those who don't have a life at all before death.

Silence for reflection

LEADER:
Jesus' third word on the cross: "Woman, behold your son: behold your Mother."

(Observe the babe)

THIRD READER:
Lord Jesus, how can we behold anything when our hearts are bound? Our eyes are open and our eyes are the window to the heart and soul. But if we are cold and untouched there, we do not really see. We have suffered but survived many losses: the loss of land, the loss of language, loss of culture, loss of values. It has been said that an Indian without land loses both the heart and the soul. All these losses of our ancestors impact upon the people we are today. They have resulted in delayed grief, alcoholism, family violence, post traumatic stress disorder—to name a few. Our souls have been blinded. With our blindness we fail to see your glory in creation and your image in every human being, including ourselves. We allow the exploitation and the degradation of your precious creation, endangering our lives and others in creation. We allow the exploitation of women and children and make them third-class citizens. We discriminate against anyone who is different from us, because they could not possibly have the same image of God as we see it. But we are all children of God through adoption by grace! Lord Jesus, restore our soul sight and help us see and feel things as they are. Help us to see and feel the truth even if it is brutal and horrifying. Help us see and feel injustice in our midst. Help us care for one another and minister to one another in truth.

Silence for reflection

LEADER:
Fourth word on the cross: "My God, my God why has thou forsaken me?"

(Women move to touch the babe, lay on hands)

FOURTH READER:
Why? What evil have they done that they should feel forsaken by their God? Have we lost our hearing as well, so that we are not able to hear the cry of misery from those who feel rejected, forsaken, and abandoned? These cries come from all over Indian Country: from the Arctic Slope, from the Yukon, from Navajoland, from the plains of the Lakota, from the Mountains and

Deserts, from the Eastern hills of the Iroquois. All over, we hear these cries. Have we tuned out the bad news and only tuned into the pleasantries? Can we hear the liberating voice of Christ who is saying to us, "Be not afraid! For I am with you always! You are not alone! I am suffering in solidarity with you! Your pain is also my pain. Your forsakenness is also my forsakenness!" You and I are one in suffering! We are not free indeed until everyone is free! Lord Jesus, help us hear your word and believe.

Silence for reflection

LEADER:
Fifth word on the cross: "I thirst."

(The babe's mouth is covered)

FIFTH READER:
Hunger and thirst—so many people of the world today are deprived of their basic human needs every day of their lives. Why? What evil have they done? Victims of famine, war, and man-made disasters. We are made to sacrifice for the rich and powerful of this country. We have been too silent. Our mouths became silent as we were forced to speak and understand a foreign tongue. We were and are in many respects still spoken to like babes. But then we began to learn the language of our oppressor, began to speak like the oppressor. Many of our words have fallen to the ground like dead leaves from the trees of autumn. We are often patronized and then seemingly pacified. Are we to suffer like lambs in silence? We who dare to speak out to speak the truth are not heard. If we are heard, we are deemed militant and ostracized by both our white and red brothers and sisters. Are we a voiceless culture? Many of us have been taught to be good little Indians: to be cute, to be harmless, and not to rock the boat.

Silence for reflection

LEADER:
Jesus' sixth word on the cross: "It is finished."

(Women move away from babe)

SIXTH READER:
Is it really finished? Is the battle won? But the struggles are far from over! Let's not rush to Easter in order to avoid and minimize our pain and our people's pain and suffering. Our heads still bow down in shame and despair, without hope and without confidence, without any sense of self-worth as beloved children of God. We are consumed with guilt and shame; we cannot even look up or lift up our eyes to pray to God. We are told many times by our own people that we are not worthy. We are told that we are losers. We are not allowed to think with our minds and ask questions so that faith may grow and mature. We have been taught to be submissive to authority, to those who know it all, to the truth interpreted by them. Reality is certainly distorted when one always looks down! Is the cry of victory premature? Yes, only if we believe that the death of Jesus is the end of the story. Yes, for those who cannot believe that you have won. Lord Jesus, help us in our disbelief. Yes, only if we believe that the death of Jesus is the end of the story.

Silence for reflection

LEADER:
Jesus' seventh word on the cross: "Father, into thy hands I commend my spirit."

(Women lower babe/cradleboard and dim lights)

SEVENTH READER:
Yes, we lay in submission; we lay in fear. We especially know very well what it means to live in fear of being abandoned, fear of losing that which we have left. Our fear comes from an imbalance of power. Someone always has power over us. Our fear has to do with someone's abuse of power and their betrayal of trust. No wonder we retreat to our villages and reservations, our homelands, to escape the madness of this country. Father, into thy hands I submit my spirit, my trust.

Silence

Lord, what shall we do with this bundled babe? Is there anyone here who is brave enough to lift up this babe, this child of God?

Help him to stand upright in our presence and the presence of God. Offer a prayer that we may always stand: not broken in spirit but empowered to love, to bless, to heal. Who is brave enough? Is anyone brave enough to lift him up?

(repeat till people come up)

FIRST READER:
Who is brave enough to unbind this child's heart? Our hearts beat to the distant drum of our ancestors—faintly at first but then stronger every time we remember to give thanks to our Creator. When the heartbeat of the people is strong, it is then that we can see and feel the truth, no matter how terrible and disconcerting. Feel your heartbeat; listen to the heart beat of those around you. Who here is brave enough to unbind this babe's heart and offer a prayer for truth and for the healing of our sorrowful hearts? Who is brave enough?

SECOND READER:
Who is brave enough to give this babe a voice that will be heard? Who speaks for the babes? What do we do when the babes speak for us? Who will give food to this babe, to nurture and sustain spiritual growth?

THIRD READER:
Who will come forth and whisper in this child's ear a prayer in your Native language? A prayer for strong, good voices for our people. Who here is brave enough? Are there others?

FOURTH READER:
Who is brave enough to free this babe's hands? To let his hands touch and feel himself and others around him. Recall the hands of Christ as they were pierced upon the cross—they still reached out for us in love, touching our minds, bodies, and spirits. When hands are free they can work for love, compassion, healing.

In our hands we possess the power to love, to kill, to be killed. "But the greatest of these is love," given to us by God and son. Hands are made for love, to become a finger of one's neighbour's hand. Who is brave enough to set these hands free and offer a prayer for love, justice, peace, and that we may embrace all of our brothers and sisters in that spirit? Who here is brave enough?

FIFTH READER:
Who is brave enough to lift this babe's tender head? To release him from the guilt and shame of all the generations. Who thinks this babe is worthy? Who wants to see this babe grow and mature to share the wisdom of the ages. Who is bold enough to lift his head and offer a prayer of home and confidence? Who will do it?

SIXTH READER:
And now the babe's feet. Unbind him; let him go. Let our people go! Who will release him to freedom to walk the path of peace and righteousness? For you have been through the way of the cross: the dark road of suffering and the valley of the shadow of death. Yet the presence of the Lord never leaves you.
You follow the footsteps of Jesus and arrived at the empty tomb this day. Rejoice!
The lord has granted you your salvation and release. Dance. There are no more bindings.

SEVENTH READER:
The Babe has been unbound by volunteers.
Jump off this cradleboard and release your future. Our future. Babe, would you please offer a prayer for our release.

Print Resources

Breaking the Silence: An Interpretive Study of Residential School Impact and Healing as Illustrated by the Stories of First Nations Individuals. Assembly of First Nations. 1994.

Dancing with a Ghost: Exploring Indian Reality, by Rupert Ross. Markham, Ontario: Octopus Publishing Group, 1992.

In the Rapids: Navigating the Future of First Nations, by Ovide Mercredi and Mary Ellen Turpel. Toronto: The Penguin Group, 1993.

Journey from Fisher River: A Celebration of the Spirituality of a People through the Life of Stan McKay, by Joyce Carlson. Toronto: United Church Publishing House, 1994.

Nation to Nation: Aboriginal Sovereignty and the Future of Canada. Diane Engelstad and John Bird, editors. Concord, Ontario: Anansi Press, 1992.

Royal Commission on Aboriginal Peoples: Special Consultation with the Historic Mission Churches. November 8-9, 1993. Ottawa, Canada. A report containing briefs from the Anglican Church of Canada, the Canadian Conference of Catholic Bishops, the Presbyterian Church in Canada, and the United Church of Canada.

The Journey: Stories and Prayers for the Christian Year from People of the First Nations. Joyce Carlson, editor. Toronto: Anglican Book Centre, 1991.

Video Resources

A number of excellent video resources have been developed through Anglican Video. Two of these *(Search for Healing* and *Dancing the Dream)* have received Silver Birch awards for excellence. All are recommended as excellent for small groups or discussion.

Dancing the Dream (time: 29:44 minutes). Produced by the Anglican Church of Canada, Anglican Video, for the Council for Native Ministries, 1993. This video documents the national Native convocation at Minaki Lodge, Ontario, August, 1993. The video gives some historical background about Native people in the Anglican Church of Canada. In between the narration of events at the convocation, some Native people speak about their painful experiences in the church, while others offer solutions for healing. The primate, Michael Peers, offers an apology to Native people on behalf of the Anglican Church of Canada for the pain inflicted. The "dancing" metaphor reflects the process of taking new and difficult steps as well as the hope that God will turn "mourning" into "dancing." Suitable for adults. A leader's guide is included.

The Seventh Fire (time: 30 minutes). Produced by Anglican Video for the Council for Native Ministries. 1995. This video outlines the history of the relationship between Aboriginal peoples and the Anglican Church of Canada. It begins with a reflection on the Hendry Report in 1969 and documents the changes of the 1970s and 1980s culminating with the Native covenant to work together with the Anglican Church of Canada to self-determination. Suitable for adults.

Search for Healing (time: 24 minutes). Produced by the Anglican Church of Canada, Anglican Video, for the Council for Native Ministries, 1992. This is a video dedicated to Canadian Native people who attended Anglican residential schools between 1829 to 1969. The video shows footage of Native children in the schools interspersed by accounts of some of the women who experienced both emotional and physical abuse while they were at the residential schools. While the program speaks of the pain inflicted, it is a search for healing for everyone involved. Suitable for use in church and school settings.

Sharing the Dream (time: 52 minutes). Produced by Anglican Video for the Council for Native Ministries. A moving record of the historic 1988 convocation when 180 Canadian Native Anglicans gathered in Fort Qu'Appelle, Saskatchewan, to share their dreams as Native people and as members of the Anglican Church of Canada. Suitable for adults.

The Dumont Brothers: Paths of the Spirit (24 minutes). Produced by the United Church of Canada, Berkely Studios. 1992. Jim and Alf Dumont are two brothers who earned theological degrees from Toronto's Emmanuel College. Alf became an ordained minister in the United Church of Canada and went on to become a Speaker of the All Native Circle Conference. Jim entered into a search for the roots of his own Native Spirituality and became a professor of Native Studies at Laurentian University in Sudbury. In the video the two brothers describe the different paths of their spiritual journeys. This poignant personal story will be of interest to those who want to draw a parallel between Traditional Spirituality and the faith experience of non-Native Christians. Suitable for adults and high school youth.

The Spirit in the Circle (time: 28 minutes). Produced by Anglican Video for the Council for Native Ministries. 1992. This video documents a gathering of First Nations people as they share insights and concerns about Native Spirituality. It is a series of moving vignettes which portray the pain and struggle of Native people in their efforts to recover the rich spiritual and cultural heritage which has been lost due to colonization. Suitable for adults and high school youth.

Who We Are: A Celebration of Native Youth (30 minutes). Produced by Minister of Supply and Services. 1992. Accompanied by a study guide in English and French. A program that features candid, action-oriented profiles of young Native people, their Elders, and other inspiring Native role models across Canada. It provides positive messages to Native youth about continuing their education, valuing their culture, and making their own unique contributions to their communities, both urban and rural. From a Haida Potlatch in B.C., to an Inuit Elder's igloo, to a Native rock concert in Quebec – Native youth are invited to share in a spirit of pride and celebrate who they are. Suitable for youth.

The Healing Circle (time: 55 minutes). Produced by Anglican Video. A chronicle of courage, pain, and spirituality. Anglican Video was granted a rare entree into the traditional, sacred healing rites of Native people as they struggled to overcome the legacy of their residential school experiences.

Over a two-year period, Anglican Video documented healing circles in Lytton, B.C., and Sioux Lookout, Ontario; recorded proceedings of the Royal Commission on Aboriginal Peoples; and conducted extensive interviews with Native leaders, including Assembly of First Nations chief Ovide Mercredi, traditional healer Seis'lom, and many others. The result is a powerful and moving documentary that testifies to the resurgence of a people's spirit.